HOMESTEAD YOUR HOUSE

Warner, Sherman & Ihara

IMPORTANT

Nolo Press is committed to keeping its books up-to-date. Each new printing, whether or not it is called a new edition, has been revised to reflect the latest law changes. This book was printed and updated on the last date indicated below. Before you rely on information in it, you might wish to call Nolo Press (415) 549-1976 to check whether a later printing or edition has been issued.

NOLO PRESS • 950 Parker St., Berkeley, CA 94710

PRINTING HISTORY

New "**Printing**" means there have been some minor changes, but usually not enough so that people will need to trade in or discard an earlier printing of the same edition. Obviously, this is a judgment call and any change, no matter how minor, might affect you.

New "**Edition**" means one or more major, or a number of minor, law changes since the previous edition.

FIRST EDITION	1973
SECOND EDITION	1975
Revised 2nd	1976
THIRD EDITION	1978
FOURTH EDITION	1981
FIFTH EDITION	September 1983
2nd Printing	November 1984
SIXTH EDITION	January 1986
2nd Printing	September 1986
3rd Printing	March 1988
SEVENTH EDITION	July 1989
ILLUSTRATIONS	Linda Allison
PRODUCTION	Stephanie Harolde
BOOK DESIGN	Jackie Clark
	Amy Ihara
INDEX	Sayre Van Young
PRINTING	Delta Lithograph

Library of Congress Catalog Card Number 89-062231
ISBN 0-87337-103-8
Copyright © 1973, 1978, 1981, 1985, 1988 & 1989 by
Ralph Warner, Charles Sherman and Toni Ihara

5
FORCED SALE BY CREDITORS

A. Real Estate 5/2
    1. Notification of the Creditor's Plans to Force a Sale
    2. The Hearing on the Order for Sale
    3. The Sale

B. Dwellings That Are Not Real Estate 5/8
    1. How to Fill Out the Claim of Exemption Form
    2. The Hearing

6
ABANDONING A DECLARED HOMESTEAD

A. Selling the Property 6/1

B. Filing a New Declaration of Homestead 6/2

C. Filing an Declaration of Abandonment 6/3
    1. Filling Out the Abandonment Form
    2. Getting the Abandonment Notarized
    3. Recording the Abandonment

7
FINDING AND HIRING A LAWYER

APPENDIX A
APPENDIX B
GLOSSARY

RECYCLE YOUR OUT-OF-DATE BOOKS & GET 25% OFF YOUR NEXT PURCHASE!

Using an old edition can be dangerous if information in it is wrong. Unfortunately, laws and legal procedures change often. To help you keep up to date we extend this offer. If you cut out and deliver to us the title portion of the cover of any old Nolo book we'll give you a 25% discount off the retail price of any new Nolo book. For example, if you have a copy of TENANT'S RIGHTS, 4th edition and want to trade it for the latest CALIFORNIA MARRIAGE AND DIVORCE LAW, send us the TENANT'S RIGHTS cover and a check for the current price of MARRIAGE & DIVORCE, less a 25% discount. Information on current prices and editions is listed in the NOLO NEWS. Generally speaking, any book more than two years old is of questionable value. Books more than four or five years old are a menace. This offer is to individuals only.

OUT OF DATE = DANGEROUS

homestead 7/89

1
HOW TO USE THIS BOOK

This book contains complete instructions on how to prepare and file a Declaration of Homestead, a document that can help protect your ownership interest (equity) in your home if creditors file claims against it. Tear-out Declaration of Homestead forms are included.

Filing a homestead is a simple process. You shouldn't need a lawyer. Following the instructions in Chapter 3 of this book should allow you to do a good job. The rest of the book provides background material on homestead protection and how a homestead actually protects your equity in your home if creditors try to take it.

Some unusual situations may require legal advice before you file. Consult a lawyer if:

- you own a house and are not sure if it is your legal residence;
- the place you are homesteading is used primarily for business purposes;
- you want to homestead a long-term lease; or
- your home is owned by a corporation rather than by you in your individual capacity.

In addition, you should always see a lawyer if a creditor is trying to force the sale of your dwelling, whether or not you have filed a Declaration of Homestead. Chapter 7 discusses how to find and hire a lawyer, should the need arise.

2

HOMESTEAD PROTECTION: AN OVERVIEW

Your equity in the house you live in—the value of your house over and above the amount you owe on it—may well be your most important material asset. You can protect all, or at least a substantial amount of that equity from current and future creditors simply by recording (filing with the County Recorder) a simple form called a "Declaration of Homestead." The declaration is a one-page form; it's easy to fill out without a lawyer's help, and the process costs only $5.

A.
How a Declaration of Homestead Works

Once you have recorded a homestead declaration, your creditors cannot force a sale of your home to pay a judgment against you unless the sale would produce enough money to:

- pay all existing liens (claims on your property),[1] **and**
- pay off mortgages and other loans secured by equity in your house; **and**
- pay the costs of selling your home, **and**

---

[1]There may be liens on your real property if you haven't paid a court judgment (a judgment lien), a contractor (a mechanic's lien) or taxes (a tax lien).

- let you keep your remaining equity in the house, up to the amount protected by the homestead ($30,000 to $75,000, depending on your filing status—see Section D below).

The only exceptions are if the creditor is trying to foreclose on the mortgage (deed of trust) on the house itself or a home equity or other loan for which you have pledged the house as security, or to collect a judgment for back child support, spousal support or taxes (see Section I below). A homestead does not protect your equity in those situations.

If you sell your house voluntarily, or if a creditor who has a court judgment on the property tries to force a sale of the house, having a recorded homestead declaration protects you in two ways:

1. You are entitled to keep a certain amount of your equity ($30,000 to $75,000, depending on your age, income and family status) from the proceeds of the sale for six months. Creditors cannot take it during that period.

2. You can keep creditors from grabbing the equity by investing it in another home, and recording a Declaration of Homestead on the new residence, within the six months.[2]

Technically, a Declaration of Homestead works by preventing a judgment lien—a lien based on a court judgment against you—from attaching to your entire equity in the home. Instead, the judgment lien "attaches" only to the portion of your equity that exceeds the amount exempted by the homestead. This means that if you have recorded a Declaration of Homestead and then voluntarily sell your home, the judgment creditor can't, through the lien, reach the portion of your equity protected by the homestead exemption.

1. Forced Sales

A judgment creditor—someone who has sued you and won a court judgment against you—is unlikely to try to force the sale of your home except as a last resort. Forcing the sale of a home is a long, drawn-out process for the creditor, who normally must hire a lawyer and pay a number of other up-front costs. Most prefer to collect their judgments by taking other property—wages, bank accounts, or other real estate. Your homestead rights, which put a certain amount of your equity off-limits to creditors, make a forced sale even more unlikely unless the portion of the home you own (your equity) is worth significantly more than the amount you owe on the mortgage (deed of trust) and any home equity loans. The forced sale process is discussed in more detail in Chapter 5. Consult a lawyer if a judgment creditor tries to force a sale of your house.

Example: Susan's home is worth $150,000, but she still owes $120,000 on the mortgage. She records a Declaration of Homestead; as a single person, she is entitled to $30,000 of

---

[2]California Code of Civil Procedure (C.C.P.) § 704.730, 704.960.

homestead protection. When Susan can't pay a department store credit card debt, the store sues her and wins. The store immediately records the judgment with the County Recorder in the county where Susan's house is located; that creates a judgment lien on Susan's house for the amount of the judgment. Later, another creditor, a loan company Susan borrowed money from on a personal loan, also sues and gets a court judgment. The loan company wants to force a sale of the house to pay off the judgment.

Because of Susan's homestead rights, the loan company cannot force a sale of the house unless the sale would bring enough to pay off the $120,000 mortgage, give Susan her $30,000 homestead amount, pay off the department store's judgment, and pay the costs of sale (at least several thousand dollars). Practically, the loan company will also want to see that at least some money will be left over to satisfy its debt.

A validly declared homestead continues to protect your equity in a house even if you no longer live in it, unless the homestead has been abandoned or you have subsequently declared a homestead on another property.

2. Voluntary Sales

A judgment creditor may record a judgment against you in the county in which your home is located, thereby creating a lien on your home, but make no attempt to force a sale. Later, if you sell your home, the lien will have to be paid off for the new buyer to take clear title to the property unless you have previously recorded a Declaration of Homestead on the house. If you have done this your creditors may not be able to touch the amount of your equity protected by homestead if you sell your house and buy another within six months.[3]

---

[3]A warning is indicated here, however. Some title companies drag their feet or refuse to clear title even if you have recorded a Declaration of Homestead prior to selling your home if you attempt to use the protected equity to purchase another

Example: *Paul and Tiffany own a house worth $180,000 and owe $120,000 on the mortgage. Their equity is thus $60,000. They have recorded a Declaration of Homestead on the house and are entitled to $45,000 of homestead protection. A creditor wins a lawsuit against them for $20,000 and records the judgment. Paul and Tiffany then sell the house for $180,000:*

- *$120,000 goes to the bank to pay off the mortgage.*
- *$45,000 goes to Paul and Tiffany. Creditors can't touch it for six months, and if Paul and Tiffany invest it in another house, they can record a new Declaration of Homestead and keep the $45,000 protected from creditors indefinitely.*
- *The remaining $15,000 goes to the creditor to cover costs of sale and pay off part of the judgment. Paul and Tiffany still owe the rest ($5,000) of the judgment.*

within six months. In short, despite the clear language of the homestead law (C.C.P. Section 704.960), these title companies try to force you to pay off judgment liens, with the equity protected by your declared homestead.

B.
What Kinds of Homes Are Protected

A Declaration of Homestead protects only dwellings that are considered real estate. In practice, that means only houses, condominiums and mobile homes that are permanently attached to land are protected.[4]

C.
Declared and 'Automatic' Homesteads

Even people who don't record a Declaration of Homestead get protection from forced sales under California's "automatic homestead" law.[5] But be warned: the automatic homestead isn't really automatic. If a creditor gets a court judgment against you and tries to force a sale of your home, you must go to court to protect your homestead rights (see Chapter 5). No one does it for you.

Here are the automatic homestead's main features:

- The amount of homestead protection is the same as with a declared homestead; it ranges from $30,000 to $75,000, depending on your circumstances. See Section D.

- Unlike a declared homestead, the automatic homestead law protects your equity in any kind of living space, not just real estate.

- The automatic homestead law does not protect your equity from creditors if you sell your home voluntarily and buy

---

[4] A homestead can also protect your equity (if any) in a long-term lease (two years or more) on residential real property. We don't discuss that kind of homestead in this book.

[5] The declared homestead law is found in Chapter 4, Article 5 of the California Code of Civil Procedure (C.C.P. § 704.910 to § 704.995). The automatic homestead law is in Chapter 4, Article 4 (C.C.P. § 704.710 to § 704.850).

another within six months, the way the declared homestead is supposed to. Unfortunately, in this situation some title companies are refusing to clear title on homes even where a declared homestead was filed before a creditor established a judgment lien. They insist that the homeowner pay off the liens. Thus, in practice there may not be much difference between the two types of homestead protection in this situation.

- To qualify for automatic homestead protection, you or your spouse must be living in the dwelling when the creditor creates a lien against the property (by recording the judgment) and continue living there at least until a judge rules on your request for the homestead protection.[6]

- And, as mentioned, if a creditor tries to get a court to authorize the sale of your home, you must go to court to prove you are entitled to the protection of the homestead law. With a recorded homestead declaration, on the other hand, the creditor must go to court to prove that your homestead is invalid in order to reach the portion of your equity that the homestead protects.

1. Boats, Motor Homes and Other Dwellings

You cannot file a Declaration of Homestead for your dwelling unless it's real estate. But the automatic homestead law protects your equity in anything used as a dwelling, including boats, other "waterborne vessels" and mobile homes. Treehouses, Winnebagos and abandoned railroad cars would also qualify if they were actually being used as your primary residence.

---

[6]C.C.P. § 704.710.

2. Selling Your Home Voluntarily

If you are relying on the automatic homestead provisions, you won't be able to sell your dwelling and get your money out of it and into another without first paying off the liens that creditors have filed against you. The technical reason for this is that whoever buys your property will not receive clear title to it unless you pay off all the liens. Unless you can promise the buyer clear title, and unless a title company will issue title insurance guaranteeing the title, the sale probably won't go through. If you have a declared homestead, however, you may be able to sell your house voluntarily without paying the judgment (see Section A).

3. Forced Sales

As mentioned, the so-called automatic homestead isn't really automatic. True, you get its protections without recording a Declaration of Homestead. But if a creditor tries to force a sale of your dwelling, you must take action to enforce your homestead protection. Forced sales of property subject to an automatic homestead are discussed in Chapter 5.

If, when a creditor tries to force the sale of your house, you and your spouse are living in separate homes, only one of your homesteads will be protected.[7] If, however, each of you has a declared homestead on your separate homes, each of you is protected.

---

[7] C.C.P. § 704.720(c).

D.
How Much Equity Is Protected

The amount of equity protected by a homestead depends on the circumstances of the homeowner when a creditor seeks to have the homesteaded house sold or the owner wants to sell it.

If you are:	Your homestead protection is:
Single	$30,000
A member of a family unit	$45,000
Over 65 or disabled (or your spouse is)	$75,000
Over 55 and your income is $15,000 or less (or $20,000, if married)	$75,000

The state legislature raises homestead exemption levels fairly regularly. If you have already recorded a Declaration of Homestead, you don't need to file a new one to be entitled to the higher amount. Your protection is automatically raised, unless the underlying debt is based on a contract (something paid for in installments or a bank loan). In this case, you get the amount of the exemption that was in effect when the debt was incurred. Non-contractual debts, such as those arising from personal injuries, however, are always subject to the latest exemption level.[8]

---

[8] *Ingrebretsen v. McNamer* (1982) 137 Cal. App. 3d 957.

Example: *You recorded a Declaration of Homestead in 1973, when the equity protection for single people was $10,000. Currently, your protection is $30,000, except for contractual debts. If you incurred a debt on a contract when the homestead protection was still $10,000, that's the maximum amount of your protection on that debt, now.*

If your equity exceeds the amount protected, your creditors may be able to force a sale of your house if it would bring enough to pay off your homestead amount, the costs of sale, and all liens and mortgages on the property. This is discussed in detail in Chapter 5.

It's possible to reduce your equity to keep it within the protected amount by refinancing the place or taking out another loan on it. A lawyer or accountant might have some ideas on the subject and should be consulted before you act.

1. Single Owners: $30,000

When one owner is listed on the Declaration of Homestead or living in the dwelling when the homestead is automatically applied, the homestead amount is $30,000. Exceptions: A debtor who is 55 years old and low-income, 65 years old, or disabled may qualify for a larger homestead amount.

2. Family Units: $45,000

If a single owner is part of a "family unit" when the court considers whether the dwelling should be sold, the homestead protection is $45,000.

The law defines "family unit" as any of the following:

1. The owner and spouse, if the two are living together;

2. The owner and any of the following people, who the owner cares for or maintains in the homestead, if these others

have no ownership in the house or own only a community property interest:

a. The minor child or minor grandchild of the owner or of the owner's present, former or deceased spouse;

b. The minor brother or sister of the owner or owner's spouse or the minor child of a deceased brother or sister of either spouse;

c. The father, mother, grandfather, or grandmother of the owner or the owner's spouse or the father, mother, grandfather, or grandmother of a deceased spouse;

d. An unmarried adult relative described in this list who is unable to take care of or support himself or herself; or

3. The owner's spouse and at least one of the people described above who the owner's spouse cares for or maintains in the homestead.[9]

Unrelated "family" members. It is clear that the legislature only intends the $45,000 exemption to apply to

---

[9] C.C.P. § 704.710.

families related by blood or marriage. Thus, even if your living arrangement is "family" in every sense of the word, if no one of the specified relatives of the home's owner is living there, the exemption is only $30,000. However, if one or more unrelated people are living together and each is a part owner, each may independently declare a homestead on his or her ownership share. Simply put, two unmarried people may get better protection than a married couple.

3. Disabled, Older or Low-Income Owners: $75,000

Homestead protection is $75,000 if:

- The judgment debtor or spouse of the judgment debtor is over 65 years old; **or**

- The judgment debtor or spouse is physically or mentally disabled and unable to work when the property is to be sold. People are presumed unable to work if they receive Social Security Disability or Supplemental Security Income benefits. However, others may be able to establish their disability as well; **or**

- The sale is involuntary, and the judgment debtor is 55 or older with a gross annual income of not more than $15,000 or, if the judgment debtor is married, the combined gross annual income of both spouses is not more than $20,000.

INCREASING HOMESTEAD PROTECTION

Homestead protection comes from the California Constitution, whose writers wanted people to have a degree of security in their homes—not live with the fear that some unexpected debt might cause them to lose it. They put this notion into the Constitution and left it to the legislature to pass laws to put it into action.

The legislature raises homestead protection amounts from time to time, but considering the current price of housing in California, the amounts are obviously too low. After you record your homestead, consider writing your State Senator and Representative and urging them to increase the amount of equity protected by the homestead. (See Appendix B for a sample letter.)

4. If Your Status Changes

If your family status or income changes after you record a Declaration of Homestead, you do not have to record a new declaration. The amount of equity protected by a homestead depends on your status—single, head of household, disabled and so on—when a creditor tries to force a sale of the homesteaded property, not when you record your Declaration of Homestead. A court will look at your circumstances when a creditor asks it to order a sale of your property, not before.

Example: *Shirley records a Declaration of Homestead when she is 45 years old. Because of her age and the facts that she lives alone and isn't disabled, she is then entitled to $30,000 of homestead protection. Eight years later, Shirley becomes disabled. Ten years later Shirley is sued for failure to pay a debt. When the judgment creditor asks a court to authorize sale of her homesteaded house, the judge rules that Shirley is* *entitled to $75,000 of homestead protection. The amount she was entitled to when she recorded her declaration is irrelevant.*

However, to be on the safe side, record a new homestead declaration if your change in family status entitles you to a higher level of protection than when you initially recorded. It's easy to do, and has an added benefit: a creditor who sees (in the public records) that you are entitled to a large homestead amount may be discouraged from trying to force the sale of your house.

If your status changes so that you are entitled to a lower amount of homestead protection, there is no reason to record a new declaration. For example, if you were part of a family unit when you recorded a declaration (entitling you to protection at the $45,000 level) but are now single, under 65 and not disabled, your original declaration is still valid, but your protection has probably decreased to $30,000.[10]

E.

Who Needs to Record a Declaration of Homestead

You should record a Declaration of Homestead if it seems likely that a creditor will sue you for a large sum of money. The declared homestead strongly discourages creditors from trying to force a sale of your home to pay off a court judgment, and it can also protect your equity if you want to sell your house and buy another. Unlike the "automatic homestead," the protections of which a homeowner may never choose to take advantage, a declared homestead tells a creditor you know your rights and will take advantage of them.

---

[10] *California Bank v. Schlesinger*(1958) 324 P.2d 119.

If you own a business that operates as a sole proprietorship or partnership, you should definitely record a declaration. Although a homestead protects only equity in your home, if your non-incorporated business is successfully sued, creditors can go after your own property, not just business assets, to pay off the judgment. If your business is a corporation, it's much harder for creditors to get to assets you own individually.[11]

F.
Who Can Record a Declaration of Homestead

Anyone who owns or is buying the place he is living in can record a Declaration of Homestead. One declaration protects a married couple and family members. However, to be fully protected, unmarried co-owners should each record a separate homestead declaration on their share of the property. This is true whether title to the property is held as joint tenants or as tenants in common.

Example: *Bill, Barbara and Molly, who aren't related by blood or marriage, live together in the house they own jointly as tenants in common. Each owns a one-third interest in the property. Each could record a separate Declaration of Homestead to protect his or her share.*

Only individuals are allowed homestead protection. Corporations do not qualify.

The person filing a homestead declaration must reside in the place being homesteaded. Legally, your residence is the

---

[11] However, if you or your spouse are the primary shareholders and officers of the corporation, it is possible that your own assets can be reached by the corporation's creditors.

place where you live and intend to go on living for the indefinite future. If you're not sure where your legal residence is—perhaps you are in the military, spend summers away from what you think of as home, or have left your home temporarily because of family problems—get advice from a lawyer. Generally, temporary absences, if you intend to return to the home, do not jeopardize homestead rights. You should definitely see a lawyer if you live in more than one place and are not sure which is your primary place of residence, if you are away from your home most of the time, or if you don't intend to stay in the place you want to homestead.

G.

When To Record a Declaration of Homestead

If you're sued, record a Declaration of Homestead immediately.

To take advantage of the protections of the declared homestead, your declaration must be recorded before a creditor actually obtains a judgment from a court and records it with the County Recorder.[12] If you do not record a declaration in time, you will be eligible only for the automatic homestead as to that debt.

For example, suppose you can't pay a good-sized debt. To collect, the creditor must first sue you and get a judgment from a court. If you have not recorded a Declaration of Homestead when the creditor records the judgment (which creates a judgment lien on your property) the creditor becomes entitled to have the judgment paid out of the proceeds if you decide to sell the house. And if the creditor tries to force the sale of your home, you will have to rely on the protection of the "automatic" homestead law (see Section C).

---

[12] C.C.P. § 704.950(a).

H.
Will Declaring a Homestead Hurt Your Credit?

Some people may tell you that recording a homestead on your home hurts your credit rating. When it comes to reputable creditors, that is simply not true. A person extending credit looks first at the borrower's ability to repay and second at the ability to repossess the property sold or taken as security. Creditors simply do not make loans relying on the possibility of later forcing the sale of the borrower's house to collect. To have a person's home sold to pay a judgment based on an unpaid bill is so much trouble, and so time-consuming (it takes months, and sometimes more than a year), that almost no lender (bail bondsmen may be an exception) plans to follow this approach.

I.
Debts Not Covered by Homestead

A homestead (either automatic or declared) will protect your home from being sold to pay off judgments that result from most kinds of debts. It makes no difference if the debt underlying the judgment is to the butcher, dressmaker, doctor, furniture store, airline, or was incurred as a result of an automobile accident. You are protected.

The following kinds of debts, however, are not covered by either an automatic or declared homestead:

1. Child Support and Alimony

The homestead laws do not protect your home against court judgments obtained for back child support or spousal support (also called alimony). The reason for this is the strong social policy in favor of making sure these obligations are met.

2. Mortgage (Deed of Trust) and Home Equity Loans

The homestead laws don't keep the wolf from your door when it is holding a mortgage (deed of trust on the homesteaded house) in its jaw. Mortgage loans and home equity loans and remodeling loans are secured by the property itself. They are exempt from the homestead laws for the obvious reason that no creditor would give you a mortgage or home equity loan in the first place unless it could sell your home if you didn't make your payments.

You need a mortgage (trust deed) to buy almost any house, but you should think twice before allowing your house to become security for other loans. This is true even though interest on home equity loans is tax deductible. Yes, it can be a bit cheaper to borrow money against your home than using credit cards or other consumer borrowing avenues, but you won't feel so smart if you borrow too much, can't repay it and lose your house as a consequence.

Some unscrupulous lenders or people who sell goods on installment contracts have been known to trick people into putting up their home as security without realizing it. When borrowing money or buying things on installments, be sure to read the contract very carefully to make sure that you do not carelessly or unintentionally sign away your place as security for a loan.

3. Taxes

The government may help protect you from other greedy creditors, but not when it comes to its own bill—it thinks there's something sacred about the money you owe for taxes. If you can't pay your tax bills, then you should know that local and county governments are usually quite slow to move toward forcing a sale of your house, and reasonable about helping you out, but watch out for the feds.[13] The IRS has been known to act rather heartlessly.

Mechanic's Lien Note: Someone who works on a house—an architect or roofer, for example—is automatically granted a mechanic's (materialman's) lien against the property to guarantee payment for the work.[14] When mechanic's liens are recorded against a house with a declared homestead, a sale cannot be forced solely on the basis of the liens.[15] However, the liens will have to be paid if the property is voluntarily sold.

---

[13] Normally, it takes five years for city and county governments to move to sell your house for non-payment of taxes. Under the Senior Citizens' Property Tax Postponement Act, many homeowners age 62 or over can postpone property taxes until death or sale of the house. Contact the Franchise Tax Board in Sacramento for more information.

[14] Civil Code § 3110.

[15] If the lien holder sues you for the money and obtains a judgment, however, a sale can be forced as part of the judgment collection process, subject to the protection afforded your equity under the homestead laws.

3
HOW TO PREPARE AND FILE A HOMESTEAD DECLARATION

This chapter contains instructions on how to fill out your Declaration of Homestead and how to record it with the County Recorder. The process is easy. Just type in the information asked for on the declaration, following our instructions, sign it in front of a notary public, and mail or take it to the County Recorder's office.

A.
Choosing the Right Form

There are two Declaration of Homestead forms in this book. Use the first form, the one for individuals, unless you and your spouse own the property jointly.

B.
Filling Out the Declaration

Sample Declaration of Homestead forms are shown below. Tear-out copies are in the back of the book.

DECLARATION OF HOMESTEAD (INDIVIDUAL)

1. I, _____, hereby declare:
2. ☐ I am declaring this homestead as an individual.

    ☐ I am a member of a family unit consisting of myself and
    _____
    _____.

3. My birthdate is: _____. My spouse's birthdate is:_____.

4. ☐ I am disabled. ☐ My spouse is disabled.

5. I now reside on that land and premises in the city of _____, County of _____, State of California, described as follows:

6. This is ☐ my ☐ my spouse's principal dwelling.
7. I hereby claim and declare these premises as a homestead for my benefit.
8. The facts stated in this declaration are true as of my personal knowledge.

Dated: _____   _____
                              Signature of Declarant

STATE OF CALIFORNIA   )
) ss
COUNTY OF _____   )

On _____, 19___, personally appeared before me, the undersigned, a Notary Public in and for the State of California, _____, personally known to me, or proved to me on the basis of satisfactory evidence, to be the persons whose name is subscribed to this instrument and acknowledged to me that _____ executed it.

Witness my hand and official seal.

_____

Notary Public

1. Declaration of Homestead (Individual)

Item 1. Put your name in the blank. Make sure that it is in the same form as your signature. For example, if in Item 1 you use the name "JOHN MILTON DOE," sign your name the same way, not "JOHN M. DOE," or "J.M. DOE." County recorders are often particular when it comes to names being exactly the same throughout.

Item 2. Check the first box if you are declaring as an individual. Check the second box if you are declaring as part of a family unit, and put the names of the family members who live with you. If you are married but own the house as your separate property, check the second box and put the name of your spouse or other individual as the person who qualifies you as a family unit. See Chapter 2, Section D.

Item 3. Fill in the appropriate birthdates. You will be entitled to a greater amount of homestead protection if you or your spouse is 65, or 55 if your income is low enough (see Chapter 2, Section D), when creditors try to force a sale of your house or you sell it voluntarily.

Item 4. If you or your spouse is disabled, check the appropriate box. See Chapter 2, Section D for the meaning of disabled.

Item 5. This part of the form asks for the location and legal description of your home. In the blanks provided, type in the name of the city and county where it's located.

If you are not within any city limits, just leave the first blank empty and, on the second blank, enter the name of the county. Following the words "described as follows:" you must copy the legal description from your deed to the property. You can find the legal description near the center of your deed, usually following the phrase "known and described as follows."

Include on your homestead declaration everything from your deed that appears to describe your property. If you have trouble finding the deed, you can get a copy of it from the County Recorder. If you are not certain which part of it is the legal description, ask a real estate or title company. Some deeds have extremely lengthy descriptions. An elaborate description may take up more space than is provided on the form. If this is the case, don't abbreviate the description but continue it on a clearly labeled second sheet of paper which can then be attached by stapling it to the first form. An additional fee will be charged for recording a second sheet.

There are three main kinds of legal descriptions of property in California:

Subdivision lot. Subdivided land is often described by reference to a lot number on a certain map on file with the County Recorder. For example, "Parcel 35 of Country View Estates, a duly recorded subdivision, a map of which was recorded in the Contra Costa County plat books at book 498, page 1213, on January 17, 1986."

Metes and bounds. This method describes the perimeter of the property. The description must thus start at an identifiable point and end there as well. Here's an example that refers to a map recorded in San Francisco:

ORDER NO. 220-596-2

The land referred to in this Report is situated in the State of California, County of City & SAN FRANCISCO, and is described as follows:

BEGINNING at a point on the northerly line of Geary Boulevard, formerly Geary Street, distant thereon 75 feet easterly from the easterly line of 44th Avenue; running thence northerly at right angles to said line of Geary Boulevard 90 feet, 1-1/4 inches to the southerly line of Point Lobos Avenue; thence easterly along said line of Point Lobos Avenue 31 feet, 10 inches; thence southerly 86 feet, 3/4 of an inch to a point on said northerly line of Geary Boulevard, distant thereon 92 feet, 4-3/8 inches easterly from the said easterly line of 44th Avenue; thence westerly along said line of Geary Boulevard 17 feet, 4-3/8 inches to the point of beginning.

BEING a portion of OUTSIDE LAND BLOCK NO. 224.

Township/Range. The third way of describing property is based on a survey system that divides the state into a grid. The north-south lines are called ranges, and the east-west lines are called townships. The starting place for a description of this kind is always one of the three north-south lines in California that are designated as "principal meridians." The space on the grid where the property is located is identified by counting from a principal meridian. Each space on the grid east or west of a principal meridian counts as one range. Confused? It gets worse. Each space on the grid created by township and range lines is divided into 36 one-square-mile sections. It's easier to understand by looking at a diagram:

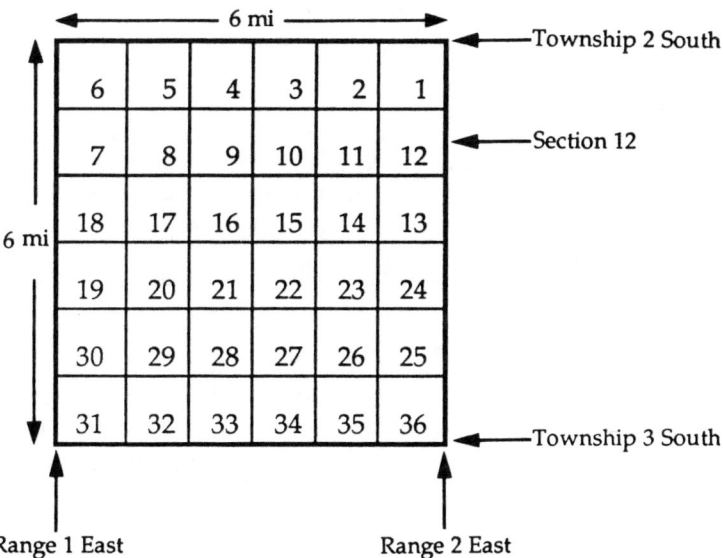

Item 6. If you use the home as your principal residence, check the first box. If your spouse does, also check the second box.

Items 7 and 8. You don't need to do anything here.

Signature: Don't sign or date the form until you take it to a Notary Public (see Section C below).

2. Declaration of Homestead (Couple)

Item 1. Put both your name and your spouse's name in the space if you are married and declaring the homestead jointly. Later, when you sign the declaration, make sure that your signature matches your typed-in name exactly. For example, if in Item 1 you use the name "JOHN MILTON DOE," sign your name the same way, not "JOHN M. DOE," or "J.M. DOE." County recorders are often particular when it comes to names being exactly the same throughout.

Item 2. You don't need to do anything here. This statement is to assure the court that you and the other person signing the declaration are married.

Item 3. Fill in the appropriate birthdates. You will be entitled to a greater amount of homestead protection if you are (or your spouse is) 65, or 55 if your income is low enough (see Chapter 2, Section D), when creditors try to force a sale of your house or you sell it voluntarily.

Item 4. If you or your spouse is disabled, check the appropriate box. See Chapter 2, Section D for the meaning of disabled.

Item 5. This part of your form contains the location and legal description of your property. In the blanks provided, type in the name of the city and county where your place is located.

DECLARATION OF HOMESTEAD (COUPLE)

1. We, _____
   _____, hereby declare:

2. We are husband and wife.

3. Husband's birthdate is: _____.

    Wife's birthdate is: _____.

4. ☐ Husband is disabled.   ☐ Wife is disabled.

5. We now reside on that land and premises in the city of
   _____, County of
   _____, State of California, described as follows:

6. This is our principal dwelling. We hereby claim and declare these premises as a homestead for our joint benefit.

7. The facts stated in this declaration are true as of our personal knowledge.

Dated: _____   _____
                            Signature of Declarant

                            _____
                            Signature of Declarant

STATE OF CALIFORNIA   )
) ss
COUNTY OF _____)

On _____, 19___, personally appeared before me, the undersigned, a Notary Public in and for the State of California, _____
_____,
personally known to me, or proved to me on the basis of satisfactory evidence, to be the persons whose names are subscribed to this instrument and acknowledged to me that they executed it.

Witness my hand and official seal.

_____
Notary Public

If you are not within any city limits, just leave the first blank empty and in the second blank, enter the name of the county. Following the words "described as follows:" type in the legal description found on your deed. Follow the instructions for Item 5 on Form 1, in section 1 above.

Items 6 and 7. You don't need to do anything here.

Signature: Don't sign or date the form until you take it to a Notary Public (Section C below).

C.
Getting the Declaration Notarized

Once you have filled out the Declaration of Homestead, it must be sworn to and signed in the presence of a Notary Public, who will charge a small amount for notarizing a document. If it is a joint declaration by husband and wife, then both must appear and sign before the notary. You will be asked to produce identification unless the notary already knows who you are. Notaries can be found at most real estate offices, county offices, law offices, banks and in many libraries. If you have a problem locating one, check the Yellow Pages of the phone book.

D.
Recording the Declaration

After the homestead declaration is signed and notarized, you can either mail it or take it to the County Recorder for the county in which your property is located. The County Recorder will make a copy of the declaration and enter it into the formal public records of your county. When the document has been recorded, it will be returned to you.

Appendix B lists all California county recorders and their addresses. The declaration must be accompanied by a money order for $5.00. If you have attached a second page, enclose the required additional amount (ask the Recorder's Office). If you mail your declaration, include a self-addressed, stamped envelope for its return. Meanwhile, it's a good idea to make a photocopy before you submit it, just in case it gets lost.

4

DEATH, DIVORCE AND BANKRUPTCY

Apart from protecting you from hungry creditors, a declared homestead has important consequences if you die, divorce or file for bankruptcy.

A. Death

A Declaration of Homestead stays in effect and protects surviving family members even if the homeowner who signed the Declaration of Homestead dies.[1] Here are some general rules that apply when an owner of a declared homestead dies.

1. Death of a Joint Owner

If one joint owner of a dwelling dies, and the other has previously independently declared a homestead on his or her interest in the property, that interest is still protected.

Example: Sam and Harry own and live in a house together. Each has recorded a Declaration of Homestead on the property. If Sam dies, Harry's homestead rights aren't affected; if a judgment creditor puts a lien on the property, or Harry wants

---

[1] C.C.P. § 704.995.

to sell his interest in the house, he is still entitled to $30,000 of equity from the proceeds.

2. Protection for Surviving Family Members

Any surviving spouse or other member of the deceased homestead owner's family will be protected under the homestead declaration if:

1. they are living in the dwelling when the homestead owner dies, and
2. they inherit all or part of the deceased owner's interest in the dwelling.

It is not necessary for the surviving person to have been listed in the Declaration of Homestead.

Example: *Ruth records a Declaration of Homestead on her house. Later, she marries Murray, who moves into the house. When Ruth dies, Murray inherits the house and continues to live there. He does not need to record a Declaration of Homestead; he is protected under the one Ruth filed.*

3. New Non-Family Member Owners

If a property owner with a declared homestead dies, and the property is left to someone other than a member of the deceased owner's family, the new owner is not protected by the old homestead declaration. The new owner must move into the dwelling and file a new declaration of homestead.

Example: *Same facts as the previous example, except that Ruth, instead of leaving her house to Murray, leaves it to her friend Naomi, who lives in another town. If Naomi wants* *homestead protection, she will have to move into the house and record a Declaration of Homestead.*

WHAT IS A PROBATE HOMESTEAD?

At the death of a property owner, the surviving spouse and minor children are automatically entitled to continue to occupy the family home.[2] When the inventory of the estate is filed with the probate court (within a few months after probate begins), the court may create a "probate homestead" to continue the protection of the family.[3] Property that is included in the probate homestead is exempt from creditors' claims that would have been subject to an automatic homestead exemption at the deceased's death.[4] A probate homestead is not the same thing as the homestead discussed in this book and does not depend on filing any papers with the County Recorder.

To create a probate homestead, the court may set apart property, including the family home, for the surviving spouse or minor children. When deciding whether or not to establish a probate homestead, the judge considers the needs of the family, the liens and encumbrances on the property, the claims of creditors, and the intent of the deceased. The probate homestead lasts a set amount of time, but never beyond the lifetime of the surviving spouse or the time the children reach majority.

---

[2] Probate Code § 6500.

[3] Probate Code § 6521.

[4] Probate Code § 6526.

B.
Divorce

The effect of divorce on homesteaded property depends on whether the property belonged to both spouses or was the separate property of just one. California community property law is quite complicated; you may want to consult *California Marriage and Divorce Law* (Nolo Press) for a much more detailed discussion.

1. Separate Property

A divorce ends any right that one spouse has in the homesteaded separate property of the other. Separate property always belongs to its owner, and the homestead gave the other spouse no ownership interest in it.

Example: Anne owns a house outright when she marries Robert. She keeps the house in her name and doesn't transfer any ownership interest in it to Robert. Anne declares a homestead as a single individual and lists Robert as a family member. They later divorce. Robert has no interest in Anne's house.

2. Community Property

A divorce does not, in and of itself, affect the homestead rights of a formerly married couple who filed a homestead declaration together for property they own jointly. Until one spouse legally transfers his or her half interest in the property to the other spouse, they still own the property together, even though they're no longer married.

Usually, when a couple divorces, one spouse signs a grant or quitclaim deed transferring his or her interest in the property to the other spouse. The deed is then recorded with the county recorder. Or, if a legal description of the property is set forth in the divorce decree, the judge may order the decree itself recorded.[5] The declared homestead still protects the interest of the spouse who continues to own the house.

If a couple owns homesteaded community property which, for some reason, is not transferred by deed or divorce decree after they divorce, the declared homestead is still valid.

C.
Bankruptcy

If you are out on a limb with too many bills and not enough income, and you want to start over, you can file for bankruptcy, as thousands of Californians do each year.[6] Your home, assuming you're living in it at the time, won't be taken by the bankruptcy court to pay your creditors unless your equity exceeds the amount protected by the homestead law plus the total of all liens and mortgages on the property.

---

[5]See Sherman, *How to Do Your Own Divorce in California* (Nolo Press).

[6]A good source of information for those over their heads in debt and facing lawsuits, attachments, bill collector harassment and the possibility of bankruptcy is *How to File for Bankruptcy*, by Elias, Renauer and Leonard (Nolo Press).

When it comes to bankruptcy your homestead protection comes from the "automatic" homestead protection discussed in Chapter 1, Section C, not as a result of declaring a homestead. However, remember that a homestead does not protect you from the mortgage holder or a holder of a loan for which the house itself has been pledged as security (e.g. a home equity loan). These creditors can foreclose if you are delinquent in payments.

Example 1: *Hannah owns a home worth $150,000 and owes $80,000 on the mortgage, giving her approximately $70,000 in equity. She has never filed a Declaration of Homestead. She files for bankruptcy. Her home will probably be taken and sold by the bankruptcy court. If the forced sale brings $140,000, the proceeds will be distributed as follows:*

$80,000 will go to the bank to pay off the mortgage;

$30,000 will go to Hannah, as her homestead amount;

$5,000 - $10,000 will go for costs of sale; and

$20,000 -$25,000 remaining will be distributed among Hannah's creditors by the bankruptcy court.[7]

Example 2: *Hannah owns the same $150,000 house but owes $100,000 on the mortgage. The bankruptcy court might well decide not to take the house and sell it, even though after the bank and Hannah are paid there still should be, at least theoretically, some money left for the creditors. That's because costs of sale, which can easily amount to $5,000 or more, must be subtracted from the proceeds remaining after the mortgage and Hannah's protected homestead amount are paid. In addition, houses rarely bring top dollar at a forced sale. So even if the market value of the house is $150,000, at a forced sale it might bring in only $130,000. If it did, nothing would*

---

[7]Property sold at a forced sale almost always brings less than it would if sold in a normal commercial transaction.

be left over for the creditors after the bank and Hannah are paid off.

Important: Let us repeat, to receive the homestead exemption in a bankruptcy proceeding, you or your spouse must be living in the home when you file for bankruptcy. If you are not living in the home, you are not entitled to the homestead exemption.[8]

Example: *Sarah and Brian file a Declaration of Homestead on their house. Later, to be closer to Brian's job, they lease that house and move to another. They don't record a new declaration on the new residence and they don't file an abandonment of the old Declaration of Homestead (Chapter 6). Shortly after they move, they file for bankruptcy. Homestead protection (in this case, under the automatic homestead law) applies only to the home they were living in when they filed for bankruptcy.*

---

[8] *In re Anderson*, 824 F.2d 754 (9th Cir. 1987).

5

FORCED SALE BY CREDITORS

If you are entitled to homestead protection, under either a Declaration of Homestead or the "automatic" homestead law, a judgment creditor cannot force the sale of your house unless the proceeds of the sale would exceed the sum of:

- the homestead amount,
- the amount still owing on mortgages on the property, and
- all liens and encumbrances against the property.[1]

First, however, the creditor must sue you and win the lawsuit. Then, if your dwelling is real estate (a conventional house, condominium, co-op, or mobile home attached to your land), the creditor must get a court order authorizing the sale. If your dwelling is personal property (a boat or motor home, for example), the creditor does not need a court order, and you will need to file a form called a "claim of exemption" with the sheriff who tries to seize the property (Section B below).

Warning: If a judgment creditor tries to force the sale of your home, see a lawyer. This chapter outlines the process, but you will need individual professional help to have the best chance of keeping your home.

---

[1] C.C.P. § 704.800(a).

REDUCING YOUR EQUITY

It may be possible to reduce your equity to keep it within the protected amount by refinancing the place or taking out another loan on it. A lawyer or accountant might have some ideas on the subject and ought to be consulted before you act.

A.
Real Estate

To force the sale of a dwelling that is real estate—a house, condominium, cooperative or mobilehome permanently situated on land—is a complicated process which, luckily, doesn't happen often. Here's an overview of the process.

1. Notification of the Creditor's Plans to Force a Sale

Any judgment creditor who wants to force a sale of real property must first get a document called a Writ of Execution from the proper court, which is routine. Then, the county sheriff or marshal will serve you with a copy of the Writ of Execution and another document called a Notice of Levy.

Within 20 days after the date of service, the creditor must ask the court for an order of sale. The creditor must supply the court with certain information: the amount of the homestead exemption, the fair market value of the property and the amount of liens and encumbrances on the property.[2]

The court will then issue a document called an Order to Show Cause, scheduling a court hearing within 45 days at which the judge will decide whether or not to issue an order authorizing the dwelling to be sold. At the hearing, you will

---

[2] C.C.P. § 704.760.

have a chance to show you are entitled to the homestead exemption (see next section).[3]

The form that you will receive, giving you notice of the hearing, is shown below.

2. The Hearing on the Order for Sale

If the application for the order for sale states the amount of the homestead exemption as being one figure (say $30,000), but you believe that it's higher ($45,000 or $75,000), then you must establish that fact—by showing that you are disabled, for example—whether the homestead is automatic or declared.[4]

If you have a declared homestead. If you filed a Declaration of Homestead on the property before the judgment was recorded with the County Recorder's Office, it's up to the creditor to convince the court, at the hearing, that the homestead is invalid in order to get the property sold on that ground.[5] This is virtually impossible to do unless there is some major defect in the homestead declaration—for example, if you weren't living in the home when you filed the declaration.

If you are relying on the automatic homestead. If you haven't filed a Declaration of Homestead on the property, it's up to you to prove that you are entitled to a certain amount of homestead protection.[6] This may not be too difficult, but the "burden of proof" is on you. If you do not prove that you are eligible for a certain amount of homestead protection (see Chapter 2, Section D), and your home is sold, your equity will not be protected from creditors. You may get nothing from the sale.

---

[3] C.C.P. § 704.770(a).
[4] C.C.P. §704.780(a)(2).
[5] C.C.P. § 704.780(a).
[6] C.C.P. § 704.780(a).

5/4   HOMESTEAD YOUR HOUSE

SHORT TITLE:	LEVYING OFFICER FILE NO	COURT CASE NO

NOTICE
IMPORTANT LEGAL NOTICE TO HOMEOWNER

1. YOUR HOME IS ABOUT TO BE SOLD TO PAY OFF YOUR DEBTS.
2. YOU MAY BE ABLE TO STOP THE SALE OR KEEP SOME OF THE MONEY FROM THE SALE. Before your home is sold, the court will have a hearing to let you prove that you or your family live there. YOU OR YOUR SPOUSE SHOULD COME TO THIS HEARING.

DATE, TIME, AND PLACE OF THE HEARING
Date: Time: Place:*

3. READ THE PAPERS THAT CAME WITH THIS NOTICE. At the hearing you will be asked about the statements in those papers.
4. The only purpose of the hearing is to decide if your home should be sold and if you qualify for a homestead exemption on the money from the sale. The purpose is NOT to decide if you owe the debts. That has already been decided.
5. You are not required to bring an attorney with you to the hearing. For your own protection, you may want to ask an attorney for advice right away.
6. If you do not own this home, this notice is not for you. PLEASE GIVE THIS NOTICE TO YOUR LANDLORD IMMEDIATELY.

AVISO
AVISO LEGAL IMPORTANTE PARA EL PROPIETARIO DE CASA

1. SU CASA ESTA A PUNTO DE VENDERSE PARA PAGAR SUS DEUDAS.
2. USTED PUEDE DETENER LA VENTA O RECIBIR PARTE DEL DINERO DE LA VENTA. Antes de la venta de su casa, habrá una audiencia en la corte para permitirle que pruebe que usted o su familia vive allí. USTED O SU CONYUGE DEBE ASISTIR A LA AUDIENCIA.

FECHA, HORA Y LUGAR DE LA AUDIENCIA
Fecha (date): Hora (time): Lugar (place):*

3. LEA LOS DOCUMENTOS QUE LLEGARON CON ESTE AVISO. En la audiencia se le harán preguntas relacionadas con las declaraciones contenidas en estos documentos.
4. La audiencia tiene solamente el propósito de decidir si su casa debe venderse y si usted es elegible a la exención de bienes de familia sobre el dinero de la venta. La audiencia NO es para decidir si usted es responsable de las deudas. Esto ya fue decidido.
5. Usted no está obligado a venir a la audiencia con un abogado. Para su propia protección, es posible que usted quiera consultar con un abogado de inmediato.
6. Si usted no es el propietario de esta casa, este aviso no es para usted. POR FAVOR, ENTREGUESELO INMEDIATAMENTE A SU ARRENDADOR.

*Specify location from Order to Show Cause

Form Approved by the
Judicial Council of California
EJ-180 (New January 1, 1985)

**NOTICE OF HEARING ON RIGHT
TO HOMESTEAD EXEMPTION**
(Enforcement of Judgment)

CCP 704.770
Post Record Catalog #EJ-180

Example: *George and Martha have never filed a Declaration of Homestead for their house. When a judgment creditor seeks a court order to force the sale of the house, George and Martha must go to the hearing on the request and prove that they are entitled to protection under the automatic homestead law. If they don't, and the house is sold, the creditor is free to take all the proceeds of the sale, after the mortgage and costs of sale are paid off, to pay the judgment.*

The judge must determine the fair market value of the property, usually with the help of an appraiser. If the judge finds that there is no homestead protection or that the value of the house exceeds the homestead amount, costs of sale, and mortgage and other pre-existing liens, she must issue an order authorizing the property to be sold.[7]

IF YOU MISS THE HEARING

Even if you, your spouse, or your attorney does not appear at the hearing, and the judge issues an order authorizing sale of your house, you may request another hearing if the failure to appear was due to mistake, excusable neglect, inadvertence, or surprise. You'll need to sign a declaration, within 10 days after you receive a copy of the court order, saying why you did not attend. You give the declaration to the sheriff, who will give it the judge, who will then schedule a hearing to see whether you deserve another chance. The law really does go out of its way to make sure you're not deprived of any homestead to which you might otherwise be entitled.

Reminder: If you haven't already, be sure to see an attorney if you get this close to losing your house.

---

[7]C.C.P. §§ 704.780(b),(d).

3. The Sale

Just because a judge authorizes a forced sale doesn't mean the property will actually be put on the market. When homesteaded property (either automatic or declared) is subjected to a forced sale, the sale cannot go through unless a bid is received which is higher than:

a) the amount of the homestead ($75,000, $45,000 or $30,000), plus

b) the amount necessary to satisfy all pre-existing liens and mortgages.

If a large enough bid is not received, then the court order is cancelled and the property cannot be placed for sale for at least another year.[8] Also, if the bid is not at least 90% of the fair market value as determined by the judge, the creditor must ask the court for permission to accept the highest bid or ask for a new sale order, which will likely mean that the house will be reappraised.[9]

If the house is sold, you will receive the homestead exemption amount (up to the amount of your equity) from the proceeds of the sale. Creditors cannot touch it for six months after you receive it.[10] If you invest the money in another dwelling within six months, you can homestead the new place and keep your equity out of the reach of creditors.

Example: Your family home is worth $100,000 and has a $20,000 first mortgage and a $5,000 second mortgage on it. A creditor sues you, gets a judgment that you don't pay and acts to have your place sold.

From the proceeds of the sale, the creditor must pay off the $25,000 in mortgages and pay you the $45,000 protected by

---

[8] C.C.P. § 704.800(a).
[9] C.C.P. § 704.800(b).
[10] C.C.P. § 704.720(b).

your homestead. Out of the remaining money ($30,000, if the house is sold for its full value), come the legal, appraisal and selling costs—a considerable sum, most likely. What's left goes to pay the judgment. If there is anything left over it goes to you.

B.
Dwellings That Are Not Real Estate

A creditor who wins a lawsuit and gets a judgment against you then gets a document called a Writ of Execution from the court clerk. The writ is given to the sheriff or marshal, who can then, subject to certain limits, take your wages, bank accounts or items of your property and turn them over to the creditor to pay off the judgment. You will be given or mailed a document called a Notice of Levy, which tells you that the creditor is having the property seized to pay the judgment.

For example, if a judgment creditor wanted to sell your houseboat, he would give the sheriff a Writ of Execution. The sheriff would show up on the dock with the writ and proceed to seize your home, intending to sell it to pay off the judgment debt.

Within ten days of the date you receive the Notice of Levy, you must take action to protect your automatic homestead rights. You are entitled to at least get your homestead amount out of the sale if you file a paper called a "Claim of Exemption" within ten days.[11] In the claim of exemption, you tell the court that the boat is exempt under the homestead law (specifically, C.C.P. Sections 704.710, 704.720, 704.730, and 704.800), and you want it returned.

Once you fill out the Claim of Exemption and deliver it to the sheriff who seized your home in the first place, the sheriff will deliver the claim to the creditor. The creditor must then set up a court hearing, notifying you of its date and place. At the hearing, a judge will determine whether or not you are entitled to the homestead exemption. You will have to show that the dwelling (the houseboat, in this example) is your principal residence and that if it is sold, you are entitled to keep the amount of your equity, up to the homestead amount —$30,000 to $75,000, depending on your status (see Chapter 2, Section D).

---

[11]C.C.P. § 703.520.

[NOT FOR WAGE GARNISHMENT]
[RETURN TO LEVYING OFFICER. DO NOT FILE WITH COURT]

ATTORNEY OR PARTY WITHOUT ATTORNEY (Name and Address):	TELEPHONE NO.:	LEVYING OFFICER (Name and Address):
ATTORNEY FOR (Name):		
NAME OF COURT, JUDICIAL DISTRICT OR BRANCH COURT, IF ANY:		
PLAINTIFF:		
DEFENDANT:		
CLAIM OF EXEMPTION (Enforcement of Judgment)	LEVYING OFFICER FILE NO.	COURT CASE NO.

Copy all the information required above (except the top left space) from the Notice of Levy. The top left space is for your name or your attorney's name and address. The original and one copy of this form must be filed with the levying officer. DO NOT FILE WITH THE COURT.

1. My name is (specify):
2. Papers should be sent to
   ☐ me.
   ☐ my attorney (I have filed with the court and served on the judgment creditor a request that papers be sent to my attorney and my attorney has consented in writing on the request to receive these papers.)
   at the address ☐ shown above ☐ following (specify):

3. ☐ I am not the judgment debtor named in the notice of levy. The name and last known address of the judgment debtor is (specify):

4. The property I claim to be exempt is (describe):

5. The property is claimed to be exempt under the following code and section (specify):

6. The facts which support this claim are (describe):

7. ☐ The claim is made pursuant to a provision exempting property to the extent necessary for the support of the judgment debtor and the spouse and dependents of the judgment debtor. **A Financial Statement form is attached to this claim.**

8. ☐ The property claimed to be exempt is
   a. ☐ a motor vehicle, the proceeds of an execution sale of a motor vehicle, or the proceeds of insurance or other indemnification for the loss, damage, or destruction of a motor vehicle.
   b. ☐ tools, implements, materials, uniforms, furnishings, books, equipment, a commercial motor vehicle, a vessel, or other personal property used in the trade, business or profession of the judgment debtor or spouse.
   c. all other property of the same type owned by the judgment debtor, either alone or in combination with others, is (describe):

9. ☐ The property claimed to be exempt consists of the loan value of unmatured life insurance policies (including endowment and annuity policies) or benefits from matured life insurance policies (including endowment and annuity policies). All other property of the same type owned by the judgment debtor or the spouse of the judgment debtor, either alone or in combination with others, is (describe):

I declare under penalty of perjury under the laws of the State of California that the foregoing is true and correct.

Date:

▶

_____ _____
(TYPE OR PRINT NAME)   (SIGNATURE OF CLAIMANT)

Form Approved by the
Judicial Council of California
EJ-160 [New July 1, 1983]

CLAIM OF EXEMPTION
(Enforcement of Judgment)

CCP 703.520
Post Record Catalog # EJ-160

1. How to Fill Out the Claim of Exemption Form

Caption: Put your name, mailing address and telephone number in the top left-hand box. Put "in pro per" after "Attorney For."

In the next box below, copy the name of the court as it is listed on the Notice of Levy served on you by the sheriff or marshal—for example, Municipal Court for the Northern District of San Mateo County, 401 Redwood Dr., Redwood City, California.

In the third box, put the plaintiff's full name (the person who got the judgment against you) and your full name (you are the defendant).

In the box on the right side of the caption, put the name and address of the levying officer—the sheriff or marshal who gave you the Writ of Execution.

Put the levying officer's file number and the court case number in the boxes below. You can get them from the Notice of Levy served on you by the sheriff or marshal.

Item 1. Put your full name here.

Item 2. Check the first box. Also check the "shown above" box unless you want notice of the court hearing to be sent to another address, in which case check the second box and put that address.

Item 3. Leave this box blank unless the real judgment debtor is someone else. If so, put that person's last known address.

Item 4. Here, provide a brief description of the property you are claiming as your homestead. For example, "My 1983 Roadway Mobilehome (Serial No. 27423) in which I reside," or "My seasprite catamaran, docked at Slip #13, Alameda, CA, in which I reside." If the property is described on the Notice of Levy, copy that description.

Item 5. Here, put "C.C.P. Sections 704.20, 704.30, and 704.800."

Item 6. Put the following statement: "I am entitled to a homestead exemption in the sum of $[__your exemption amount__] out of the proceeds of the sale of this property, because the property is the principal residence and dwelling of [__name of your spouse or any person who makes up your family unit__], and me now and at the time the judgment in this action was recorded with the County Recorder."

If you don't have room for this statement on the form, type it on a clean 8 1/2" by 11" piece of paper, label it "Attachment, Claim of Exemption, Item 6," and attach it to the main form. Under item 6, write "continued on Attachment."

Items 7, 8, and 9. Leave all these items blank.

Signature and Date. Date the form, print or type your name on the left, and sign on the right.

Make at least two photocopies, and, within ten days of the date you were served with the Notice of Levy, deliver the original and one copy to the sheriff or marshal who served you. Keep one copy for your own records.

2. The Hearing

After you give these documents to the sheriff or marshal, the creditor will have ten days to file an opposition to your claim of exemption with the sheriff or marshal. If this isn't done, your claim will succeed, and you will receive your homestead amount if the property is sold. Most likely, though, it won't be sold unless the sale would bring more than your homestead amount, costs of sale and existing encumbrances and liens.

If the creditor does oppose your claim of exemption, you will receive two documents from the creditor: a "Notice of Opposition to Claim of Exemption," which states why the creditor opposes your homestead claim, and a "Notice of Hearing on Right to Homestead Exemption," which tells you when and where the hearing will be held.

You may want to get an attorney to help you with the hearing, but you are probably safe enough representing yourself if your claim is straightforward. You must be prepared to establish:

1. The amount of homestead exemption to which you are entitled; and

2. That you live in the living space in question and did so when the judgment was filed. The creditor may not even contest this point, but you should be ready to prove that it is your home. Some pictures of the inside of the living space might be helpful. Also, you can bring some friends or neighbors who can testify on your behalf. Be sure the judge knows that your witnesses are present.

If the judge rules in your favor, you are entitled to receive your equity, up to the homestead amount, from the proceeds of the sale. If the creditor does force a sale, no creditor can touch the money you receive for six months from the date you receive it.

If within six months you put the money into a new home in which you actually reside, the new home is automatically homesteaded. In addition, the exemption date on the new home is the date you started to reside in your old exempt home. This means the homestead protects you from judgment liens recorded since you or your spouse resided in your old home.

6

ABANDONING A DECLARED HOMESTEAD

You can only have one declared homestead at a time. If after you record a Declaration of Homestead you sell your interest in the homesteaded property, record a new Declaration of Homestead on other property, or record a Declaration of Abandonment, the first declared homestead is no longer in effect, at least as far as you are concerned.[1]

Bankruptcy note: If you file for bankruptcy, you are entitled to homestead protection only on the equity in the home you're living in when you file for bankruptcy, even if you have a declared homestead on another house. (See Chapter 4.)

A.
Selling the Property

If you sell your interest in homesteaded property as part of a commercial sale to a stranger, you clearly have no property left to protect.

However, selling or giving homesteaded community property to your spouse does not mean the homestead is automatically abandoned. It merely converts the property into

---

[1] C.C.P. §§ 704.980, 704.990.

the separate property of your spouse, and your spouse keeps the protection of the original homestead.

B.
Filing a New Declaration of Homestead

If you move out of a place where you have a declared homestead and file a new homestead declaration on another place, you abandon your homestead protection in the first home.

If just one of two or more co-owners files a new declaration, it has no effect on any other person named in the prior homestead declaration, unless they are also named in the new declaration.

Example: Tom and Jane, an unmarried couple who have filed a homestead declaration on their home, break up. Tom moves out and files a new homestead declaration on his new dwelling for himself only. Jane's interest is still protected (for $30,000 or $45,000, depending on who else lives with her), but Tom's is automatically abandoned. It would also be automatically abandoned if Tom sold his interest in the house.

C.
Filing an Declaration of Abandonment

Generally, you don't need to record a Declaration of Abandonment of Homestead, since the law automatically considers your homestead abandoned when you file a new declaration on different property or when you sell the homesteaded property. There are some potentially confusing situations, however, when it may make sense to abandon one homestead when you record another. For example, if you own two or more houses and move back and forth, formally abandoning one homestead when you file another can help keep the record straight.

A Declaration of Abandonment must be recorded in the same County Recorder's office as the Declaration of Homestead was recorded.

1. Filling Out the Abandonment Form

Item 1. Fill in the name(s) of the person(s) making the declaration. There is room for two names so that a husband and wife who joined in a homestead may now join in its abandonment. An individual may also use this same form. Be consistent in the use of your name. Use exactly the same form of your name you used on the homestead declaration, and stick to that form throughout. For example: the name "JOHN MILTON DOE" should not later appear as "JOHN M. DOE."

DECLARATON OF ABANDONMENT OF HOMESTEAD

1. I (we) _____, do hereby declare:

2. ☐ I (wey abandon the homestead heretofore declared by me (us) on _____, 19___, on those premises known and described as follows:

the declaration of which homestead was recorded on _____, 19___, in Book _____, Page _____, of the _____ records of _____ County, California.

Dated: _____   _____
                         Signature of Declarant

                         _____
                         Signature of Declarant

STATE OF CALIFORNIA   )
) ss
COUNTY OF _____   )

On _____, 19___, personally appeared before me, the undersigned, a Notary Public in and for the State of California, _____, personally known to me, or proved to me on the basis of satisfactory evidence, to be the persons whose names are subscribed to this instrument and acknowledged to me that they executed it.

Witness my hand and official seal.

_____
Notary Public

Item 2. The first blanks of Item 2 are filled in with the date on which the homestead declaration was signed. This is followed by the legal description of the property, exactly as it appeared on the Declaration of Homestead. The last blanks are for the recording information, which can usually be found on the original document, stamped on the upper or lower margin of the document. It shows the date of recordation and the Book and Page numbers of the county records into which it was entered.

If you have lost your original Declaration, you can obtain a copy from the County Recorder for the county in which the declaration was filed.

2. Getting the Abandonment Notarized

You must now sign and date the document in front of a Notary Public. If two people sign the document, both signatures must be notarized. There is usually a small fee for notarizing each signature. You can probably find a notary in a real estate or insurance office, bank or library—or look in the Yellow Pages of the phone book.

3. Recording the Abandonment

Mail or hand deliver the notarized Abandonment to the County Recorder of the county in which the original Declaration of Homestead was filed, along with a money order for $5.00 to cover the recording fee. Appendix A contains a list of all County Recorders in California. If you mail the Abandonment, include a self-addressed, stamped envelope so the County Recorder can return the document to you. When you get it back, save it for your files.

7

FINDING AND HIRING A LAWYER

With the help of this book, most people will find it easy to complete and record a Declaration of Homestead. But if you have difficulty, or if a creditor tries to force a sale of your home, you will very likely want to consult a lawyer.

Finding a lawyer who is knowledgeable about protecting your home in the judgment collection process, charges reasonable prices and whom you trust is not always an easy task. Think about these options:

Legal Aid. If you have a very low income, you may qualify for free legal help from your local Legal Aid Office. Check your phone directory for its location, or ask the County Clerk.

Legal Clinics. Law clinics such as Hyatt Legal Services and Jacoby & Meyers loudly advertise their low initial consultation fees. This generally means that a basic consultation is cheap, often about $20; anything beyond that isn't so cheap. Often, the trick for you is to quickly get your questions answered and resist any attempt to convince you that you need further services. But if the lawyer you talk to is experienced with debtors' problems, and you're comfortable with the lawyer and the representation, it may be worth it to pay for a full consultation to get more information and advice. However, if you are told you need an expensive procedure it will probably be wise to get a second opinion.

Group Legal Plans. Many groups, including unions, employers and consumer action groups, now offer legal plans to their members. Under a few, you get legal protection free of charge. If so, take advantage of it. Under others, members can get legal assistance for rates that are supposed to be lower than lawyers in private practice usually charge, but in reality may not be. Some of these plans are good, but many funnel you to run-of-the-mill lawyers with no special competence in the area of your concern who charge pretty close to the going rate.

Prepaid Legal Insurance. It's a misnomer to call these programs, which provide an initial level of service for a low fee and then charge specific fees for additional work, legal insurance. Most prepaid plans are more a marketing device for the participating lawyers than they are insurance plans.

The plans are sold by companies such as the Bank of America, Montgomery Ward and Amway. They are often offered to credit card holders or sold door to door. There's no guarantee that the lawyers available through these plans are of the best caliber; sometimes they aren't.

If you join a prepaid legal insurance plan that offers extensive free advice and you have a homestead problem, take advantage of the free consultation. But be forewarned: The lawyer is probably getting only $2 or $3 per month from the plan for dealing with you, and may have agreed to this minimal amount in the hope of snaring people into paying for extra legal services not covered by the monthly premium. So be wary—if the lawyer recommends an expensive legal procedure not covered by what you have already paid, get a second opinion before you agree.

Private Attorneys. The best way to find a good lawyer is to get a recommendation from a satisfied client. Ask a friend who has a small business; chances are he or she has a satisfactory relationship with an attorney.

If you can't get a reliable recommendation from a friend, you'll have to shop around on your own. Here are some suggestions to make your search easier:

- Check with a local consumer organization to see if it can recommend someone.
- Be wary of referral panels set up by local bar associations. Most lawyers can get on these panels by paying a fee if they have been in practice for a short time. Membership on most of these panels normally demonstrates little or no special competence in the particular area of law for which a referral is given—it often means no more than that the attorney needs work. In addition, many referral systems charge you for the referral which you might better get free elsewhere.
- Shop around by calling different law offices and stating your problem. Ask how much it would cost for a visit. Try to talk to a lawyer personally to attempt to get an idea of how friendly and sympathetic he or she is to your concerns.
- Remember, lawyers whose offices and life styles are reasonably simple are more likely to help you for less money than lawyers who work in the tower suite of the tallest building in town. You should be able to find an attorney willing to discuss your problems for $75 to $125. Even that amount may seem high, but it's worth it if your house is at stake.

- Check the attorney advertisements in the Yellow Pages of the phone book and the classified ad section of your newspaper. Look for someone who claims, at least, to have experience with real estate and judgment collection matters.

APPENDIX A

Mail or take your form, along with $5.00, to the County Recorder for your county.

ALAMEDA
Room 100 Courthouse
1225 Fallon Street
Oakland, CA 94612

ALPINE
Box 266
Markleeville, CA 96120

AMADOR
108 Court Street
Jackson, CA 95642

BUTTE
Administration Bldg.
25 County Center Dr.
Oroville, CA 95965

CALAVERAS
Government Center
San Andreas, CA 95249

COLUSA
929 Bridge St.
Colusa, CA 95932

CONTRA COSTA
Courthouse
730 Las Juntas
Martinez, CA 94553

DEL NORTE
450 H Street
Crescent City, CA 95531

EL DORADO
360 Fair Lane
Placerville, CA 95667

FRESNO
2281 Tulare
Fresno, CA 93721

GLENN
P.O. Box 391
Willows, CA 95988

HUMBOLDT
Courthouse
825 5th Street
Eureka, CA 95501

IMPERIAL
P.O. Box 1560
940 Main St.
El Centro, CA 92244

INYO
P.O. Drawer F
Independence, CA 93526

KERN
1655 Chester Ave.
Bakersfield, CA 93301

KINGS
1400 W. Lacey Blvd.
Hanford, CA 93230

LAKE
Courthouse
255 North Forbes St.
Lakeport, CA 95453

LASSEN
Courthouse
Lassen St.
Susanville, CA 96130

LOS ANGELES
New Hall of Records
227 North Broadway
Los Angeles, CA 90012

MADERA
209 W. Yosemite Ave.
Madera, CA 93637

MARIN
Civic Center
Hall of Justice
San Rafael, CA 94903

MARIPOSA
Box 156
Mariposa, CA 95338

MENDOCINO
Box 148
Room 6 Courthouse
Ukiah, CA 95482

MERCED
2222 M Street
Merced, CA 95340

MODOC
P.O. Box 850,
Courthouse
Alturas, CA 96101

MONO
Box 537
Courthouse
Bridgeport, CA 93517

MONTEREY
Box 29
Salinas, CA 93902

NAPA
Hall of Records
1195 3rd Street
Napa, CA 94559

NEVADA
950 Maidu Ave.
P.O. 6100
Nevada City, CA 95959

ORANGE
630 N. Broadway,
Room 101, Box 238
Santa Ana, CA 92702

PLACER
175 Fulweiler Ave.,
Room 101
Auburn, CA 95603

PLUMAS
Box 10706
Quincy, CA 95971

RIVERSIDE
4080 Lemon St.
Box 751
Riverside, CA 92502

SACRAMENTO
901 G Street
Sacramento, CA 95814

SAN BENITO
Room 206 Courthouse
Hollister, CA 95023

SAN BERNARDINO
172 W. 3rd St.
Second Floor
San Bernardino, CA 92415

SAN DIEGO
1600 Pacific Hwy.
Room 260
P.O. Box 1750
San Diego, CA 92112

SAN FRANCISCO
Room 167 City Hall
San Francisco, CA 94102

SAN JOAQUIN
24 S. Hunter, Rm. 304
Stockton, CA 95202

SAN LUIS OBISPO
County Government Center,
Room 102
San Luis Obispo, CA 93408

SAN MATEO
Hall of Justice & Records
Redwood City, CA 94063

SANTA BARBARA
P.O. Drawer CC
Santa Barbara, CA 93102

SANTA CLARA
70 W. Hedding St.
San Jose, CA 95110

SANTA CRUZ
701 Ocean Street
Room 230
Santa Cruz, CA 95060

SHASTA
Courthouse, Room 102
Redding, CA 96001

SIERRA
P.O. Drawer D
Downieville, CA 95936

SISKIYOU
Box 8
Yreka, CA 96097

SOLANO
Courthouse
Fairfield, CA 94533

SONOMA
585 Fiscal Drive,
Room 103, Box 6124
Santa Rosa, CA 95406

STANISLAUS
P.O. Box 1008
Modesto, CA 95354

SUTTER
Hall of Records
466 2nd Street
Yuba City, CA 95991

TEHAMA
Courthouse
Box 250
Red Bluff, CA 96080

TRINITY
P.O. Box 1258
Weaverville, CA 96093

TULARE
203 Courthouse
Visalia, CA 93291

TUOLOMNE
28 N. Lower Sunset Drive
Sonora, CA 95370

VENTURA
800 S. Victoria Avenue
Ventura, CA 93009

YOLO
625 Court Street, Rm. 105
P.O. Box 1820
Woodland, CA 95695

YUBA
Courthouse
P.O. 1389
Marysville, CA 95901

APPENDIX B

Where to Write to Demand Increased Homestead Protection

The homestead law exists because the Constitution of the State of California says it must. It exists to protect you. Ideally, homestead protection should be automatic. Filing of a homestead declaration should not be required, and everyone who owns or is buying a home should be protected. Certainly it is not fair for people to end up with reduced protection just because they did not know how to get a homestead on file.

Writing your state legislators asking that the homestead protection be made truly automatic, and the protection amounts increased, may focus the attention of the California legislature on expanding homestead protections. Here is an example of a letter you can send to your state representatives:

1500 Acorn St.
Cloverdale, CA
June 1, 19__

Dear Senator or Assemblyperson _____:

I believe that legislation should be passed to automatically extend homestead protections to anyone who owns or is buying a home. The present so-called automatic homestead law is not adequate to do this, because it provides less protection than the declared homestead law. All Californians should have the security of not having their homes sold from under them, as was the original intention of the homestead provision of the California State Constitution.

Legislation should also be introduced to raise the amounts protected. As our money becomes worth less and less, existing protection amounts become more and more inadequate. I feel that a family should be entitled to a good, solid home, free of the threat of a forced sale. At least $100,000 of equity in a home should be protected.

Many Californians would benefit from any action taken in these directions. Thank you for your consideration of this letter.

Sincerely,

Elizabeth Gray

GLOSSARY

County Recorder: The county official who keeps records of all transfers affecting real estate in the county. A Declaration of Homestead must be filed (recorded) with the County Recorder for the county in which the property is located.

Court judgment: See **Judgment**.

Creditor: Someone to whom you owe money. See also **Judgment creditor.**

Declaration of Homestead: The form you record (file) with the county recorder to establish a declared homestead for your home.

Dwelling: Under the homestead laws, dwelling has two different meanings. For the purpose of the "automatic homestead" law (discussed in Chapter 2), a dwelling is any place owned by you where you actually reside. It includes houses (and surrounding land and outbuildings), mobile and motor homes, boats, condominiums, planned developments, stock cooperatives and community apartment projects.

For the purpose of declaring a homestead, however, the term "dwelling" refers only to a personally-owned home which is also considered real estate. Thus, for example, houses, condominiums and mobile homes which are permanently placed on land qualify as dwellings for purposes of declaring a homestead. A boat or motor home does not, because it isn't attached to real estate.

Equity: The amount of your home that you actually own. It is figured by taking what you could get for your home if you sold it (the fair market value) and subtracting the costs of sale and the pay-off on any loans secured by the property—in particular, the mortgage. For example, if your home could be sold for $100,000, you owe $70,000 on your mortgage, and it would cost $5,000 to sell it (counting the real estate agent's commission and other costs), then your equity is $25,000.

Forced Sale: If you owe money and don't pay it, a creditor may get a court order authorizing it to put your home up for sale to pay off the debt. A creditor must sue you, win and get permission from the court before it can force the sale of your home.

Homestead (Automatic): The so-called automatic homestead protects the dwelling in which a debtor lives continually from the time a creditor files a judgment lien against the property until the case actually gets to court and a judge approves the debtor's homestead claim.

For example, if a creditor gets a $50,000 court judgment against Tom, the law protects Tom's equity in his house, even though Tom has never filed a formal Declaration of Homestead, as long as Tom continues living there. However, if Tom is not living in the dwelling when the foreclosure action is brought, or moves out before a judge approves of the homestead, he has no protection at all under the Automatic Homestead Law.

The automatic homestead is established by article 4 of Chapter 4 of the California Code of Civil Procedure (sections 704.710 through 704.850).

Homestead (Declared): If you file a Declaration of Homestead with the County Recorder before a creditor creates a lien on your home, a certain amount of the equity you have in your home is protected from creditors when your property is sold, either voluntarily or involuntarily.

This legal protection is found in Article 5 of Chapter 4 of the California Code of Civil Procedure (sections 704.910 through 704.995).

Judgment: If a creditor brings a lawsuit against someone and wins, the creditor gets a judgment from the court. The judgment against the debtor, now called a "judgment debtor," is for a certain amount of money. It entitles the creditor to collect that money from the judgment debtor by proceeding to have the sheriff seize and sell certain of the debtor's property.

Judgment Creditor: Any person or entity who has won a lawsuit in a court and obtained a court judgment against someone.

Judgment Debtor: Someone who has lost a lawsuit and owes money on a court judgment.

Judgment Lien: After a creditor wins a lawsuit against you and gets a court judgment, the creditor can record (file) a copy of the court judgment against you with the County Recorder. Recording the judgment automatically places a claim, or lien, on your property. If your house is sold, buyers and title companies usually insist that liens must be paid off so the new owner can take title to the property free of any legal claims.

A Declaration of Homestead prevents a judgment lien from attaching to your property, except to the amount of your equity that exceeds your homestead amount. If your equity doesn't exceed that amount, you will be able to sell your property and reinvest in another home without having to first pay off the judgments.

Mechanic's Lien: Someone who works on a house—an architect or roofer, for example—is automatically granted a mechanic's or materialman's lien against the property to guarantee payment for the work. To enforce the lien, the contractor must record a claim of lien, usually within 90 days after the work is completed. When the property is sold, the lien must be paid off for the new owner to receive clear title to the property.

Personal property: All property that isn't **real property**.

Recording: All documents that affect real estate are recorded—that is, copies are made and put in the public records of the county where the real estate is located. Examples of documents that are recorded are deeds, Declarations of Homestead and mortgages.

Real property: Real property (also called real estate) is land and things permanently attached to land. Houses, barns, land and condominiums are all examples of real property.

INDEX

Alimony, and homesteading, 2/18
Appraisal of property, 5/5
Attorneys. See Lawyers
Automatic homestead, 2/14; and bankruptcy, 4/6-7; features, 2/6-7; and forced sale, 2/8, 5/3, 5/5, 5/8

Bankruptcy, and homestead, 4/5-7
Bankruptcy, 6/1
Bids, for forced sale of real estate, 5/6
Boats, as dwellings, 2/7
Business, and homestead protection, 2/15

Child support, and homesteading, 2/18
Claim of Exemption form, 5/8-11; sample, 5/9
Co-owners: and death of one, 4/1-2; and Declaration of Homestead form, 3/3-8; and new Declaration of Homestead, 6/2
Community property, 4/4-5
Corporation, and homestead protection, 2/15
Credit, and homesteading, 2/17
Creditors: and homestead exemption amount, 5/6. See also Forced sale; Judgment creditors

Death of homestead owner, 4/1-3
Debts: non-contractual, 2/9; not covered by homestead, 2/18-19
Declaration of Abandonment of Homestead, 6/3-5; fee, 6/5; filling out, 6/3, 6/5; notarization, 6/5; recording, 6/5; sample, 6/4
Declaration of Homestead form, 2/1-5: for couples, 3/3-8; fee, 3/9; filing a new one, 6/2; filling out, 3/1, 3/3-6, 3/8; for individual, 3/1-6; notarization, 3/8-9; reasons for recording, 2/14-15; recording, 3/9; samples, 3/2, 3/7; selection of, 3/1; when to record, 2/16; who can record, 2/15-16
Declared homestead, 2/6-7; abandoning, 6/1-5. See also Declaration of Homestead form

Deed of trust, and homesteading, 2/18-19
Disabled owners, and amount of homestead protection, 2/9, 2/12
Divorce, and homestead, 4/4-5
Dwelling, definition, 2/7, 5/2
Dwellings that aren't real estate, and forced sale, 5/1, 5/7-12

Equity: amount protected, 2/9-14; definition, 2/1; protection of, 2/1-5, 2/9-14; reducing, 5/2

Fair market value, of property, 5/5
Family units: definition, 2/10-11; and amount of homestead protection, 2/9, 2/10-12
Forced sale, of dwellings that aren't real estate, 5/1, 5/7-12
Forced sale, 2/2-4, 4/6n; and automatic homestead, 2/8, 5/3, 5/5, 5/8; by creditors, 5/1-7; of dwellings that aren't real estate, 5/1, 5/7-12

Group legal plans, 7/2

Hearing on order for sale, 5/3-5; of dwellings that aren't real estate, 5/11-12
Hearing on right to homestead exemption, missed, 5/5
Home equity loans, and homesteading, 2/18-19
Homes, types protected, 2/6, 2/7
Homestead protection: amount of, 2/9-14; and change in status, 2/13-14; and increase by legislature, 2/13; overview, 2/1-19

Installment contracts, 2/19

Joint owners. See Co-owners
Judgment creditor, definition, 2/3. See also Forced sale
Judgment lien, 2/3

Lawyers, 1/1, 7/1-4
Legal aid, 7/1
Legal clinics, 7/1
Legal residence: and bankruptcy, 4/7; definition, 2/15-16; and homesteading, 2/16, 5/12
Liens, 2/1, 2/19
Low-income owners, and amount of homestead protection, 2/9, 2/12

Mechanic's lien, 2/19
Metes and bounds, 3/4
Mortgage, and homesteading, 2/18-19
Motor homes, as dwellings, 2/7

New non-family owners, and death of homestead owner, 4/2-3
Notarization: of Declaration of Abandonment of Homestead, 6/5; of Declaration of Homestead form, 3/8-9
Notice of Hearing on Right to Homestead Exemption, 5/11; sample, 5/4
Notice of Levy, 5/2; and forced sale of dwellings that aren't real estate, 5/7-8
Notice of Opposition to Claim of Exemption, 5/11

Older owners, and amount of homestead protection, 2/9, 2/12
Order for sale, 5/2-5
Order to Show Cause, 5/2

Personal property, and forced sale, 5/1, 5/7-12
Prepaid legal insurance, 7/2
Probate homestead, 4/3
Property descriptions, 3/3-5

Quitclaim deed, 4/4-5

Sale, forced. See Forced sale
Selling homesteaded property, 6/1-2
Senior Citizen's Property Tax Postponement Act, 2/19n
Separate property, 4/4
Single owners, and amount of homestead protection, 2/9, 2/10
Subdivision lot, 3/4
Surviving family members, and death of homestead owner, 4/2

Taxes, and homesteading, 2/19
Township/range, 3/5

Unmarried people, and amount of homestead protection, 2/12
Unrelated family members, and amount of homestead
    protection, 2/11-12

Voluntary sale, of real estate, 2/2-3, 2/4-5; and automatic
    homestead, 2/8

Writ of Execution, 5/2; and forced sale of dwellings that aren't
    real estate, 5/7-8

SELF-HELP LAW BOOKS & SOFTWARE

SOFTWARE

willmaker
Nolo Press/Legisoft
Recent statistics say chances are better than 2 to 1 that you haven't written a will, even though you know you should. WillMaker makes the job easy, leading you step by step in a fill-in-the-blank format. Because writing a will is only one step in the estate planning process, WillMaker comes with a 200-page manual providing an overview of probate avoidance and tax planning techniques.
National 3rd Ed.
Apple, IBM PC 5 1/4 & 3 1/2,
Macintosh $59.95
Commodore $39.95

california incorporator
Attorney Mancuso and Legisoft, Inc.
About half of the small California corporations formed today are done without the services of a lawyer. This easy-to-use software program lets you do the paperwork with minimum effort. Just answer the questions on the screen, and California Incorporator will print out the 35-40 pages of documents you need to make your California corporation legal.
California Edition (IBM) $129.00

the california nonprofit corporation handbook—computer edition with disk
Attorney Anthony Mancuso
This is the standard work on how to form a nonprofit corporation in California. Included on the disk are the forms for the Articles, Bylaws and Minutes you will need, as wel as regular and special director and member minute forms. Also included are several chapters with line-by-line instructions explaining how to apply for and obtain federal tax exempt status. This is a critical step in the incorporation of any nonprofit organizaton and applies to incorporating in all 50 states.
California 1st Ed.
IBM PC 5 1/4 & 3 1/2 $69.00
Macintosh $69.00

for the record
Attorney Warner & Pladsen
A book/software package that helps to keep track of personal and financial records; create documents to give to family members in case of emergency; leave an accurate record for heirs, and allows easy access to all important records with the ability to print out any section.
National 1st Edition
Macintosh, IBM PC 5 1/4 & 3 1/2 $49.95

how to form your own new york corporation—computer edition with disk
Attorney Anthony Mancuso
More and more business people are incorporating to qualify for tax benefits, limited liability status, the benefit of employee status and financial flexibility. This software package contains all the instructions, tax information and forms you need to incorporate a small business, including the Certificate of Incorporation, Bylaws, Minutes and Stock Certificates. The 250-page manual includes instructions on how to incorporate a new or existing business; tax and securities law information; information on S corporations; Federal Tax Reform Act rates and rules; and the latest procedures to protect your directors under state law. All organizational forms are on disk.
New York 1st Ed.
IBM PC 5 1/4 & 3 1/2 $69.00
Macintosh $69.00

how to form your own texas corporation—computer edition with disk
Attorney Anthony Mancuso
This new software package not only contains all the instructions, tax information and forms (on disk) you need to incorporate a small business, it also adds and important new element—forms for director and share holder meeting minutes, necessary for holding future meetings and transacting ongoing business. The computer edition includes:

- The Certificate of Incorporation, Bylaws, Minutes and stock certificates
- Full instructions on how to incorporate a new or already existing business
- Tax, corporation and securities law information
- Complete information on electing S Corporation tax status
- Federal Tax Reform Act rates and rules
- The latest procedures to protect your directors under state law
- And minute forms necessary for director and shareholder meetings.

Texas 1st Ed.
IBM PC 5 1/4 & 3 1/2 $69.00
Macintosh $69.00

BUSINESS

the california nonprofit corporation handbook
Attorney Anthony Mancuso
This book explains all the legal formalities involved in forming and operating a non-profit corporation. Included are all the forms for the Articles, Bylaws and Minutes you will need. Also included are complete instructions for obtaining federal 501(c)(3) exemptions and benefits. The tax information in this section applies wherever your corporation is formed.
California 5th Ed. $29.95

how to form your own corporation
Attorney Anthony Mancuso
More and more business people are incorporating to qualify for tax benefits, limited liability status, the benefit of employee status and the financial flexibility. These books contain the forms, instructions and tax information you need to incorporate a small business.
California 7th Ed. $29.95
Texas 4th Ed. $24.95
New York 2nd. Ed. $24.95
Florida 1st Ed. $19.95

1988 calcorp update package
Attorney Anthony Mancuso
This update package contains all the forms and instructions you need to modify your corporation's Articles of Incorporation so you can take advantage of new California laws. $25.00

the california professional corporation handbook
Attorney Anthony Mancuso
Health care professionals, marriage, family and child counsellors, lawyers, accountants and members of certain other professions must fulfill special requirements when forming a corporation in California. This edition contains up-to-date tax information plus all the forms and instructions necessary to form a California professional corporation. An appendix explains the special rules that apply to each profession.
California 3rd Ed. $29.95

nolo's small business start-up
Mike McKeever
Should you start a business? Should you raise money to expand your already running business? If the answers are yes, this book will show you how to write an effective business plan and loan package.
National 3rd Ed. $17.95

marketing without advertising
Michael Phillips & Salli Rasberry
Every small business person knows that the best marketing plan encourages customer loyalty and personal recommendation. Phillips and Rasberry outline practical steps for building and expanding a small business without spending a lot of money.
National 1st Ed. $14.00

the partnership book
Attorneys Clifford & Warner
Lots of people dream of going into business with a friend. The best way to keep that dream from turning into a nightmare is to have a solid partnership agreement. This book shows how to write an agreement that covers evaluation of partner assets, disputes, buy-outs and the death of a partner.
National 3rd Ed. $18.95

the independent paralegal's handbook: how to provide legal services without going to jail
Attorney Ralph Warner
A large percentage of routine legal work in this country is performed by typists, secretaries, researchers and various other law office helpers generally labeled paralegals. For those who would like to take these services out of the law office and offer them at a reasonable fee in an independent business, attorney Ralph Warner provides both legal and business guidelines.
National 1st Ed. $12.95

getting started as an independent paralegal (two audio tapes)
Attorney Ralph Warner
This set of tapes, approximately three hours in all, is a carefully edited version of Nolo Press founder Ralph Warner's Saturday Morning Law School class. It is designed for people who wish to go into business helping consumers prepare their own paperwork in uncontested actions such as bankruptcy, divorce, small business incorporations, landlord-tenant actions, probate, etc. The tapes are designed to be used in conjunction with *The Independent Paralegal's Handbook*.
National 1st Ed. $24.95

MONEY MATTERS

collect your court judgment
Scott, Elias & Goldoftas
After you win a judgment in small claims, municipal or superior court, you still have to collect your money. Here are step-by-step instructions on hwo to collect your judgment from the debtor's bank accounts, wages, business receipts, real estate or other assets.
California 1st Ed. $24.95

make your own contract
Attorney Stephen Elias
If you've ever sold a car, lent money to a relative or friend, or put money down on a prospective purchase, you should have used a contract. Here are clearly written legal form contracts to: buy and sell property, borrow and lend money, store and lend personal property, make deposits on goods for later purchase, release others from personal liability, or pay a contractor to do home repairs.
National 1st Ed. $12.95

social security, medicare & pensions
Attorney Joseph L. Matthews & Dorothy Matthews Berman
Social security, medicare and medicaid programs follow a host of complicated rules. Those over 55, or those caring for someone over 55, will find this comprehensive guidebook invaluable for understanding and utilizing their rightful benefits.
National 4th Ed. $15.95

everybody's guide to small claims court
Attorney Ralph Warner
So, the dry cleaner ruined your good flannel suit. Your roof leaks every time it rains, and the contractor who supposedly fixed it won't call you back. This book will help you decide if you have a case, show you how to file and serve papers, tell you what to bring to court, and how to collect a judgment.
California 8th Ed. $14.95
National 3rd Ed. $14.95

billpayers' rights
Attorneys Warner & Elias
Lots of people find themselves overwhelmed by debt. The law, however, offers a number of legal protections for consumers and Billpayers' Rights shows people how to use them. Areas covered include: how to handle bill collectors, deal with student loans, check your credit rating and decide if you should file for bankruptcy.
California 8th Ed. $14.95

RESEARCH & REFERENCE

legal research: how to find and understand the law
Attorney Stephen Elias
A valuable tool for paralegals, law students and legal secretaries, this book provides access to legal information. Using this book, the legal self-helper can find and research a case, read statutes, and make Freedom of Information Act requests.
National 2nd Ed. $14.95

family law dictionary
Attorneys Leonard and Elias
Written in plain English (as opposed to legalese), the Family Law Dictionary has been compiled to help the lay person doing research in the area of family law (i.e., marriage, divorce, adoption, etc.). Using cross referencs and examples as well as definitions, this book is unique as a reference tool.
National 1st Edition $13.95

patent, copyright & trademark: intellectual property law dictionary
Attorney Stephen Elias
This book uses simple language free of legal jargon to define and explain the intricacies of items associated with trade secrets, copyrights, trademarks and unfair competition, patents and patent procedures, and contracts and warranties.—IEEE Spectrum
If you're dealing with any multi-media product, a new business product or trade secret, you need this book.
National 1st Ed. $19.95

LANDLORDS, TENANTS & HOMEOWNERS

for sale by owner
George Devine
In 1986 about 600,000 homes were sold in California at a median price of $130,000. Most sellers worked with a broker and paid the 6% commission. For the median home that meant $7,800. Obviously, that's money that could be saved if you sell your own house. This book provides the background information and legal technicalities you will need to do the job yourself and with confidence.
California 1st Ed. $24.95

homestead your house
Attorneys Warner, Sherman & Ihara
Under California homestead laws, up to $60,000 of the equity in your home may be safe from creditors. But to get the maximum legal protection you should file a Declaration of Homestead before a judgment lien is recorded against you. This book includes complete instructions and tear-out forms.
California 7th Ed. $8.95

the landlord's law book: vol. 1, rights & responsibilities
Attorneys Brown & Warner
Every landlord should know the basics of landlord-tenant law. This volume covers: deposits, leases and rental agreements, inspections (tenants' privacy rights), habitability (rent withholding), ending a tenancy, liability, and rent control.
California 2nd Ed. $24.95

the landlord's law book: vol. 2, evictions
Attorney David Brown
Even the most scrupulous landlord may sometimes need to evict a tenant. In the past it has been necessary to hire a lawyer and pay a high fee. Using this book you can handle most evictions yourself safely and economically.
California 2nd Ed. $24.95

tenants' rights
Attorneys Moskowitz & Warner
Your "security building" doesn't have a working lock on the front door. Is your landlord liable? How can you get him to fix it? This book explains the best way to handle your relationship with your landlord and your legal rights when you find yourself in disagreement.
California 10th Ed. $15.95

the deeds book: how to transfer title to california real estate
Attorney Mary Randolph
The Deeds Book shows you how to choose the right kind of deed, how to complete the tear-out forms, and how to record them in the county recorder's public records. It also alerts you to real property disclosure requirements and California community property rules, as well as tax and estate planning aspects of your transfer.
California 1st Ed. $15.95

IN AND OUT OF COURT

dog law
Attorney Mary Randolph
There are 50 million dogs in the United States—and, it seems, at least that many rules and regulations for their owners to abide by. *Dog Law* covers topics that everyone who owns a dog, or lives near one, needs to know about disputes, injury or nuisance.
National 1st Ed. $12.95

the criminal records book
Attorney Warren Siegel
The Criminal Records Book takes you step by step through the procedures to: seal criminal records, dismiss convictions, destroy marijuana records, reduce felony convictions.
California 2nd Ed. $14.95

fight your ticket
Attorney David Brown
At a trade show in San Francisco recently, a traffic court judge (who must remain nameless) told our associate publisher that he keeps this book by his bench for easy reference. If you think that ticket was unfair, here's the book showing you what to do to fight it.
California 3rd Ed. $16.95

how to change your name
Attorneys Loeb & Brown
This book explains how to change your name legally and provides all the necessary court forms with detailed instructions on how to fill them out.
California 4th Ed. $14.95

FAMILY, FRIENDS & LOVERS

how to do your own divorce
Attorney Charles E. Sherman
This is the book that launched Nolo Press and advanced the self-help law movement. During the past 17 years, over 400,000 copies have been sold, saving consumers at least $50 million in legal fees (assuming 100,000 have each saved $500—certainly a conservative estimate).
California 15th Ed. $14.95
Texas 2nd Ed. $12.95

california marriage & divorce law
Attorneys Warner, Ihara & Elias
For a generation, this practical handbook has been the best resource for the Californian who wants to understand marriage and divorce laws. Even if you hire a lawyer to help you with a divorce, it's essential that you learn your basic legal rights and responsibilities.
California 10th Ed. $15.95

practical divorce solutions
Attorney Charles Ed Sherman
Written by the author of *How to Do Your Own Divorce* (with over 500,000 copies in print), this book provides a valuable guide both to the emotional process involved in divorce as well as the legal and financial decisions that have to be made.
California 1st Ed. $12.95

how to adopt your stepchild in california
Frank Zagone & Mary Randolph
For many families that include stepchildren, adoption is a satisfying way to guarantee the family a solid legal footing. This book provides sample forms and complete step-by-step instructions for completing a simple uncontested adoption by a stepparent.
California 3rd Ed. $19.95

how to modify and collect child support in california
Attorneys Matthews, Siegel & Willis
California has established landmark new standards in setting and collecting child support. Payments must now be based on both objective need standards and the parents' combined income.
Using this book, custodial parents can determine if they are entitled to higher child support payments and can implement the procedures to obtain that support.
California 2nd Ed. $17.95

the guardianship book: how to become a child's guardian in california
Lisa Goldoftas & Attorney David Brown
Thousands of children in California are left without a guardian because their parents have died, abandoned them or are unable to care for them. *The Guardianship Book* provides step-by-step instructions and the forms needed to obtain a legal guardianship without a lawyer. The book covers:

- how to prepare, file and have your guardianship papers served
- how to get a guardianship hearing set in court
- what to say to the judge
- the legal responsibilities and duties of a guardian
- information about dealing with a variety of institutions and agencies
- alternative forms for use when a legal guardianship is not needed.

California 1st Ed. $19.95

legal guide for lesbian and gay couples
Attorneys Curry & Clifford
In addition to its clear presentation of "living together" contracts, A Legal Guide contains crucial information on the special problems facing lesbians and gay men with children, civil rights legislation, and medical/legal issues.
National 5th Ed. $17.95

the living together kit
Attorneys Ihara & Warner
Few unmarried couples understand the laws that may affect them. Here are useful tips on living together agreements, paternity agreements, estate planning, and buying real estate.
National 5th Ed. $17.95

ESTATE PLANNING & PROBATE

nolo's simple will book
Attorney Denis Clifford
We feel it's important to remind people that if they don't make arrangements before they die, the state will give their property to certain close family members. If there are nieces, nephews, godchildren, friends or stepchildren you want to leave something to, you need a will. It's easy to write a legally valid will using this book, and once you've done it yourself you'll know how to update it whenever necessary.
National 1st Ed. $14.95

plan your estate: wills, probate avoidance, trusts & taxes
Attorney Denis Clifford
A will is only one part of an estate plan. The first concern is avoiding probate so that your heirs won't receive a greatly diminished inheritance years later. This book shows you how to create a "living trust" and gives you the information you need to make sure whatever you have saved goes to your heirs, not to lawyers and the government.
National 1st Ed. $17.95

the power of attorney book
Attorney Denis Clifford
The Power of Attorney Book concerns something you've heard about but probably would rather ignore: Who will take care of your affairs, make your financial and medical decisions, if you can't? With this book you can appoint someone you trust to carry out your wishes.
National 2nd Ed. $17.95

how to probate an estate
Julia Nissley
When a close relative dies, amidst the grieving there are financial and legal details to be dealt with. The natural response is to rely on an attorney, but that response can be costly. With *How to Probate an Estate* you can have the satisfaction of doing the work yourself and saving those fees.
California 3rd Ed. $24.95

JUST FOR FUN

29 reasons not to go to law school
Ralph Warner & Toni Ihara
Filled with humor and piercing observations, this book can save you three years, $70,000 and your sanity.
3rd Ed. $9.95

murder on the air
Ralph Warner & Toni Ihara
Here is a sure winner for any friend who's spent more than a week in the city of Berkeley…a catchy little mystery situated in the environs and the cultural mores of the People's Republic.—The Bay Guardian
Flat out fun.—San Francisco Chronicle
$5.95

poetic justice
Ed. by Jonathan & Andrew Roth
A unique compilation of humorous quotes about lawyers and the legal system, from Socrates to Woody Allen.
$8.95

PATENTS, COPYRIGHTS & TRADEMARKS

how to copyright software
Attorney M.J. Salone
Copyrighting is the best protection for any software. This book explains how to get a copyright and what a copyright can protect.
National 2nd Ed. $24.95

legal care for your software
Attorneys Daniel Remer & Stephen Elias
If you write programs you intend to sell, or work for a software house that pays you for programming, you should buy this book. This step-by-step guide for computer software writers covers copyright laws, trade secret protection, contracts, license agreements, trademarks, patents and more.
National 3rd Ed. $29.95

patent it yourself
Attorney David Pressman
You've invented something, or you're working on it, or you're planning to start...Patent It Yourself offers help in evaluating patentability, marketability and the protective documentation you should have. If you file your own patent application using this book, you can save from $1500 to $3500.
National 2nd Ed. $29.95

the inventor's notebook
Fred Grissom & Attorney David Pressman
The best protection for your patent is adequate records. The Inventor's Notebook provides forms, instructions, references to relevant areas of patent law, a bibliography of legal and non-legal aids, and more. It helps you document the activities that are normally part of successful independent inventing.
National 1st Ed.
$19.95

nolo
SELF-HELP LAW BOOKS & SOFTWARE

ORDER FORM

Quantity	Title	Unit Price	Total

Sales Tax (CA residents only):

7% Alameda, Contra Costa, San Diego, San Mateo & Santa Clara counties
6 1/2% Fresno, Inyo, LA, Sacramento, San Benito, San Francisco & Santa Cruz counties
6% All others

Subtotal _____

Sales Tax _____

TOTAL _____

Method of Payment:

☐ Check enclosed
☐ VISA   ☐ Mastercard
Acct #_____ Exp._____
Signature_____
Phone (   )_____

Ship to:
Name _____
Address_____
_____

Mail to:

**NOLO PRESS
950 Parker Street
Berkeley CA 94710**

For faster service, use your credit card and our toll-free numbers:

Monday-Friday 8-5 Pacific Time
US   1-800-992-6656
CA   (outside 415 area)   1-800-445-6656
       (inside 415 area)   1-415-549-1976
General Information   1-415-549-1976

Prices subject to change
Please allow 1-2 weeks for delivery
Delivery is by UPS; no P.O. boxes, please

ORDER DIRECT AND WE PAY POSTAGE & HANDLING!

NOLO PRESS
Homestead Your House Registration Card

We would like to hear from you. Please let us know if the book met your needs. Fill out and return this card for a FREE one-year subscription to the *Nolo News*, our quarterly newspaper (if you have already paid for a subscription, we will extend it for one year). It contains an update section which will keep you abreast of any changes in the law relevant to *Homestead Your House*. You'll find interesting articles on a number of legal topics, book reviews, our ever popular lawyer joke column, and a complete catalog of all Nolo books and software. In addition, we'll notify you when we publish a new edition of *Homestead Your House*. (This offer is good in the U.S.only.)

Name _____ Comments: _____
Address _____ _____
City _____ State _____ Zip _____ _____
Your occupation_____ _____
Did you record a Declaration of Homestead using this book? _____
 _____ Yes _____ No _____ Plan to
Did you find the information in the book helpful?
 (extremely helpful) 1 2 3 4 5 (not at all)
Where did you hear about the book? _____
Have you used other Nolo books? _____ Yes, _____ No
Where did you buy the book? _____

affix
postage
here

NOLO PRESS
950 Parker Street
Berkeley CA 94710

ABOUT NOLO PRESS

It's no secret that our legal system offers most Americans poor access to justice. Especially when it comes to relatively straightforward legal tasks, many people knew that too often lawyers charge too much, explain too little, and provide inadequate services.

Nolo Press, founded in 1971, pioneered a different approach: helping people gain the knowledge necessary to cope with their own routine legal problems. Nolo now publishes over 60 self-help law books and software programs. Our materials are affordable, they explain—in plain English—what the law says, and they show readers how to complete many routine legal tasks (including court appearances) without a lawyer.

Bar associations thundered against Nolo's first book, How To Do Your Own Divorce in California, claiming it was a "danger to consumers." In the next few years the public was repeatedly warned that doing your own legal paperwork, for even the simplest legal task, was akin to doing your own brain surgery. Fortunately, consumers took a hard look at the expensive alternatives the legal profession offered, examined Nolo books, and made up their own minds. Today, close to 60% of the uncontested divorces in California are done without lawyers, most of them with the help of Nolo's divorce book, which has sold close to half a million copies.

In the late 1970s, after publishing a dozen successful California self-help law books in areas as diverse as tenants' rights and incorporating a small business, Nolo broadened its focus to the whole country. We now have national books on wills, patents, estate planning, and partnerships, to mention just a few. In 1981 Nolo began publishing a quarterly self-help law newspaper, the Nolo News—Access to Law. It keeps readers up-to-date on law changes that affect our books, encourages new self-help approaches, and provides consumer information.

An important part of Nolo's purpose is to spread the word that our legal system can easily be made more affordable, accessible, and fair if it is redesigned to serve consumers instead of the legal profession. To take but one example, Nolo has repeatedly urged that competent non-lawyers (independent paralegals) be permitted to provide reasonably-priced legal form completion services.

More recently, Nolo expanded into self-help legal software with a number of easy-to-use programs, including WillMaker (with Legisoft). With over 100,000 sold, it's fair to estimate that WillMaker has made more wills than any law firm in history.

Currently, we're busy creating new programs, writing new books, and keeping our existing titles up to date. Nolo has grown from a home-base business with a couple of part-time employees to one that employs close to 50 people.

One thing that hasn't charged since Nolo's undeniably humble beginnings is our commitment to quality. Our books and software are as clear, accurate, up-to-date and useful as we can make them. To help with this process we enclose a tear-out feedback card in this book and urge you to take a minute to give us the benefit of your suggestions. Every suggestion is read by a Nolo author or editor.

When recorded return to:
_____
_____

DECLARATION OF HOMESTEAD (INDIVIDUAL)

1. I, _____, hereby declare:

2. ☐ I am declaring this homestead as an individual.
   ☐ I am a member of a family unit consisting of myself and _____.

3. My birthdate is: _____.
   My spouse's birthdate is: _____.

4. ☐ I am disabled. ☐ My spouse is disabled.

5. I now reside on that land and premises in the city of _____, County of _____, State of California, described as follows:
   _____.

6. This is ☐ my ☐ my spouse's principal dwelling.

7. I hereby claim and declare these premises as a homestead for my benefit.

8. The facts stated in this declaration are true as of my personal knowledge.

Dated: _____

_____
Signature of Declarant

STATE OF CALIFORNIA)
) ss
COUNTY OF _____)

On _____, 19___, personally appeared before me, the undersigned, a Notary Public in and for the State of California, _____, personally known to me, or proved to me on the basis of satisfactory evidence, to be the persons whose name is subscribed to this instrument and acknowledged to me that _____ executed it.

Witness my hand and official seal.

_____
Notary Public

When recorded return to:

_____
_____
_____
_____

DECLARATION OF HOMESTEAD (COUPLE)

1. We, _____, hereby declare:

2. We are husband and wife.

3. Husband's birthdate is: _____;
   Wife's birthdate is: _____.

4. ☐ Husband is disabled.   ☐ Wife is disabled.

5. We now reside on that land and premises in the city of _____, County of _____, State of California, described as follows:

6. This is our principal dwelling. We hereby claim and declare these premises as a homestead for our joint benefit.

7. The facts stated in this declaration are true as of our personal knowledge.

Dated: _____

_____
Signature of Declarant

_____
Signature of Declarant

STATE OF CALIFORNIA)
) ss
COUNTY OF _____)

On _____, 19___, personally appeared before me, the undersigned, a Notary Public in and for the State of California, personally known to me, or proved to me on the basis of satisfactory evidence, to be the persons whose names are subscribed to this instrument and acknowledged to me that they executed it.

Witness my hand and official seal.

_____
Notary Public

When recorded return to: _____

_____

DECLARATION OF ABANDONMENT OF HOMESTEAD

1. I (we) _____, do hereby declare:

2. ☐ I (we) abandon the homestead heretofore declared by me (us) on _____, 19___, on those premises known and described as follows:

   the declaration of which homestead was recorded on _____, 19___, in Book _____, Page _____, of the records of _____ County, California.

   Dated: _____

   _____
   Signature of Declarant

   _____
   Signature of Declarant

STATE OF CALIFORNIA)
COUNTY OF _____) ss
)

On _____, 19___, personally appeared before me, the undersigned, a Notary Public in and for the State of California, _____ personally known to me, or proved to me on the basis of satisfactory evidence, to be the persons whose names are subscribed to this instrument and acknowledged to me that they executed it. Witness my hand and official seal.

_____
Notary Public